Transportation in Cities

Pergamon Titles of Related Interest

Related Journals*

*Free specimen copies available upon request.

Transportation in Cities

E.O. Pederson

Pergamon Press

New York • Oxford • Toronto • Sydney • Frankfurt • Paris

388.4
P37t

Pergamon Press Offices:

U.S.A.	Pergamon Press Inc., Maxwell House, Fairview Park, Elmsford, New York 10523, U.S.A.
U.K.	Pergamon Press Ltd., Headington Hill Hall, Oxford OX3 0BW, England
CANADA	Pergamon of Canada, Ltd., Suite 104, 150 Consumers Road, Willowdale, Ontario M2J 1P9, Canada
AUSTRALIA	Pergamon Press (Aust.) Pty. Ltd., P.O. Box 544, Potts Point, NSW 2011, Australia
FRANCE	Pergamon Press SARL, 24 rue des Ecoles, 75240 Paris, Cedex 05, France
FEDERAL REPUBLIC OF GERMANY	Pergamon Press GmbH, Hammerweg 6, Postfach 1305, 6242 Kronberg/Taunus, Federal Republic of Germany

Library of Congress Cataloging in Publication Data

Pederson, Eldor Olin.
  Transportation in cities.

  (Habitat texts)
  Bibliography: p.
  Includes index.
  1. Urban transportation. 2. Land use,
Urban. 3. Underdeveloped areas—Urban transporta-
tion. I. Title. II. Series.
HE305.P43 1980   388.4   79-22726
ISBN 0-08-024666-4

Printed in the United States of America

Contents

Preface

The facilities which now exist, of
moving bodies from place to place
are amongst the curses of the
country, the destroyers of industry,
of morals, and, of course, of
happiness. (Italics in original.)
William Cobbett,
Rural Rides, 1832

With a slight change of vocabulary, Cobbett's words sound
very much like commentary on contemporary urban
transportation systems. In fact Cobbett was talking about the
condition of roads and highways in rural England, conditions
which were vastly improved in his lifetime and have seen even
greater improvements since. Cobbett did not much like cities,
describing London as a "smoky wen" in one of his writings,
but he was certainly cognizant of transportation problems
within them. What he did not foresee is that his comments
about rural transportation would be rendered untrue by
nineteenth- and twentieth-century technological improvements.
In the process, problems of urban transportation would become
more acute, and form the major transportation problem of
twentieth-century societies of the Western world.

Cobbett's complaint still rings true of transportation
conditions in the rural Third World, but even in those poorer
nations, urban transportation has become a critical problem.
In all of the world's nations, save those too small or too
primitive to have cities, urban transportation is a critical
issue. The time and money required for necessary urban
travel eat into scarce personal resources, while construction,
maintenance, and operation of roads, railroads, and other
transportation modes devour huge chunks of governmental
budgets. Air pollution, energy consumption, and visual blight
are environmental problems directly associated with
transportation and its use. Transportation is essential for the

maintenance of human life and certainly for the existence of cities, but it imposes huge costs on societies and individuals. Finding ways of achieving transportation goals while minimizing those costs is a major task for experts, governments, and concerned citizens.

This book deals with some aspects of transportation in cities, emphasizing the relationships between transportation and land uses in urban areas. The initial chapter deals with the historical context of urban development and the importance of transportation to the evolution of cities. It makes the point that for much of human history, the predominant transportation problem was the movement of goods, while today the problem is the movement of people. The second chapter examines the relationships between transportation patterns and land-use patterns in cities. Changes to land use are inevitable when transportation changes and vice versa; similarly, the form of the city is strongly related to the type of transportation which dominates it. The next two chapters deal with specific transportation problems in wealthy nations and in Third World countries. In wealthy nations, the problems arise from an unwillingness to recognize the connections between land use and transportation, while in Third World cities, population growth and poverty combine to make provision of any type of transportation difficult. Chapter 5 talks about the future relationships between transportation and land use in cities. While radical changes in transportation modes are widely discussed, they are unlikely to have much impact on cities. In fact the radical changes which are likely are changes in land use as cities adapt to the dominant transportation mode, the automobile. The final chapter outlines some projects and ideas for students of urban transportation as they attempt to analyze and evaluate urban transportation systems.

Transportation analysis is a field replete with jargon. While it is easy to rail at the use of jargon in the social sciences, those who wish to become familiar with the literature in fields like urban transportation must also learn the meaning of at least some technical terms. Sometimes words which appear to be jargon are, in reality, terms much more precise than their close synonyms of daily speech. A glossary is appended defining the terms used in the book.

In the genesis of any book, many people other than the author play a role, though all faults in the final entity remain with the author. I would like to thank my colleagues and students (past and present) for their comments and criticisms which were essential in the formulation of my ideas. I would also like to thank The George Washington University for a sabbatical leave during the 1977-78 academic year which allowed me to travel to a number of cities in Europe and Asia and to devote time to the preparation of this book.

1 Transportation and Cities: A Historical Perspective

THE IMPORTANCE OF TRANSPORTATION

Urban transportation problems are as old as cities. It is startling to read documents from ancient Rome complaining about traffic jams. The reports could be describing modern Rome. Congestion, noise, dirt, and odors were problems associated with transportation, and the city authorities attempted to mitigate them by banning wheeled traffic from some streets and from the entire city during the busiest times of the day. This was necessary so that city residents could get to work and do their shopping. Besides, there were not enough parking spaces for the oxen!

Cities are creatures of transportation. By definition cities do not feed themselves, and they can survive only when food is brought to them from rural areas. Once inside the city, the food must be distributed to the urban population. After the food has been consumed, waste materials must be collected and removed. To pay for the food, urban residents must produce something, and urban manufacturing requires raw materials, distribution of products, and removal of wastes. Cities were not possible until transportation allowed the necessary movements of food, raw materials, products, and waste.

In addition to the movement of commodities and goods, cities require the movement of people. In ancient Rome, there was a conflict between the movement of goods and the movement of people. Carts and pack animals moved materials into and out of the city. On the Roman streets, they competed with pedestrians going to work, to shop, or for entertainment. Visitors to the casbahs and bazaars of Islamic cities in West Asia and North Africa see the kind of congestion

1

that was common in ancient Rome as pack animals, carts, and pedestrians all try to use the same narrow streets.

Ancient Rome was unique among early cities, for its large size led to severe conflicts between the movement of goods and passenger transportation. The difficulties of bringing in food and raw materials and removing wastes kept most early cities small in population, while the difficulties of distribution within the cities kept their land areas small. Even though the narrow streets were often congested, the distances between activities in most early cities were short and quickly travelled.

For many centuries following the decline of Rome, the western world did not contain large cities. In Asia and Islamic Africa large cities persisted, suffering the same transportation problems endemic in ancient Rome. In Europe it was not until the late Middle Ages and the renaissance of commerce that cities comparable to Rome reappeared, bringing back problems of urban transportation. While their commercial success and artistic achievement still dazzle us, most of the cities of Renaissance Europe were smaller in population and much smaller in land area than such present day cities as Yakima, Washington in the United States or Scunthorpe in England.

Most Medieval and Renaissance cities in Europe were located on waterways. In Venice, Amsterdam, Bruges, and other places the canals served a dual transportation role. Materials were moved into and out of those cities along the waterways, and much travel within the cities was along those routes. In cities along fresh water bodies, the lakes, canals, and rivers were a source of water and a sewage removal system. Diseases which bred in the wastes and the water (cholera, malaria, typhoid, and typus the most malevolent of the diseases), helped to limit urban growth. As late as 1800 only a few European cities exceeded 100,000 residents.

Improvements to land and water transportation during the nineteenth century made it possible to bring vastly larger quantities of materials into cities, making vastly larger cities possible. At the beginning of the century, only a few cities had more than 100,000 residents or covered more than twenty-five square kilometers. By 1900 cities of over a million inhabitants were found in several nations, cities larger than 100,000 people were common, and many of those cities covered more than 500 square kilometers of land each.

Prior to 1800, the most important urban transportation problems were related to moving materials, especially food and water. Transportation improvements between 1800 and 1900 almost erased those problems but introduced the problem of moving large numbers of people over long distances within cities. Today the chief urban transportation problem is moving people to and from their homes to work, to shop, to be entertained, and to take advantage of urban services. The movement of people in cities has proved a difficult and expensive problem for contemporary societies in all parts of the world.

TRANSPORTATION TO THE CITY

The need to import food and raw materials served as a limit on the size of early cities. The high costs of transportation made long distance movement unusual except for the rarest and most valuable materials. Salt, an essential human nutrient, was the only common material to move long distances. Humans cannot live without small amounts of salt in their diets, and salt is not available at many inland locations otherwise favorable for settlement. Because it is essential, people have been willing to pay high prices for salt, though the quantities demanded have been small. The combination of high price and small quantity made long distance movement feasible as salt was transported from coastal areas and salt mines to markets.

A few other materials shared with salt the ability to pay the high costs of long-distance transportation, notably gems, precious metals, and spices. Several early cities were dependent on trade in these exotic and luxurious materials. Much romance surrounds the early history of this long-distance trade, but movements of gems, gold, and spices can be overemphasized. The trades employed few people, and except for salt, the goods traded were consumed only by the very rich.

Common foodstuffs and raw materials were rarely moved more than a few tens of kilometers from farm, forest, or mine into cities. Most cities were dependent upon land within 100 kilometers of the city wall for food, fiber, and fuel. Forests were the most important source of fuel and building material, and large amounts of land close to European cities were used for forestry. Unlike salt, wood was demanded in large quantities and was not worth much per kilogram. Wood had to be produced within a few kilometers of the city, for it was too expensive to move it over greater distances. The transport cost was a large part of the total cost of wood in cities.

All transportation available to early cities was slow and expensive, but water transportation was faster, more reliable, and less demanding of energy than land transportation. Whenever possible, cities depended on water transportation, and it is no accident that most of the world's large cities developed close to major water bodies. Cities located on navigable water had access to larger food and raw material supplies than landlocked places and could thus expand to larger size. Ancient Rome was able to feed its large population (estimated at between 100,000 and 1 million people) because of its location near the "crossroads of the Mediter-

ranean." Military control of the Mediterranean basin, and the
water transportation provided by the sea to the port of Ostia
a few kilometers from Rome, made it possible for the city to
command a huge food supply. It has been argued that Rome
fell mainly as a result of a reduction in its food supply.

> Every city, however brilliant . . . had to draw its
> food supplies from an area contained within a radius
> of about 30 kilometers. . . . If Venice was a well
> fed city, it was because her network of waterways
> enabled her to bring everyday foodstuffs and sheep
> cheese from as far off as . . . Lombardy.(1)
>
> - Fernand Braudel

Like ancient Rome, eighteenth-century London was able to
grow thanks to its water connections to supplies of food and
raw material. The navigable Thames gave access to fertile
agricultural areas inland from London, and it was an opening
to the English Channel and the Atlantic. With its water
connections, London was able to draw materials from most of
Britain, from coastal Europe, and eventually from vast colonial
holdings overseas. The supply of food and materials allowed
London's population to exceed 1 million before 1800.

Longshoremen in eighteenth-century London unloaded
cargoes from most of the world's seaports, but the city was
still primarily dependent on food grown in the Thames Valley.
Those who dislike British cooking can blame its character on
the need to use locally grown produce. The fruits and
vegetables which added variety to Mediterranean cuisines could
not be grown in England's damp and cool climate, and they
could not be transported in edible form to Britain. Only the
least perishable of foods, such as sugar, grain, wine, dried
fish, and salted meat, could be moved long distances.

During the eighteenth century, there was a slow but
pronounced improvement in water transportation. Sailing ships
became larger, faster, and more reliable. Navigation hazards
along major rivers and coastlines were marked or removed.
Technical improvements led to better navigation tools, not the
least of which were better hydrographic charts (maps). In
some places where navigation had been difficult or impossible,
canals were constructed. By 1800 many kilometers of
navigable canals had been built in England, France, and the
Low Countries. Navigation improvements made it possible to
carry greater quantities of goods over longer distances in
shorter times and for less labor and energy. They increased
the food and raw-material supplies and increased the market
areas of cities like London, Paris, and Amsterdam.

Increases in urban food and raw-material supplies were
more dramatic during the nineteenth century. Improvements
to ocean vessels led to ever greater speed and capacity,

especially after steam replaced wind as the motive power. Late
in the century, refrigeration allowed for the first time the
long-distance movement of perishable materials. One of the
first uses of refrigerated ships was to carry Argentinian beef
to Europe.

Improvements to water transportation were apparent as
early as 1750, but there were few advances in land
transportation from Roman times to almost 1800. Early in the
nineteenth century, there was a road building craze in parts
of England and the United States accompanied by minor
improvements to carriages and other road vehicles, but these
did not result in much greater speed or capacity. The
introduction of the railroad after 1825 radically transformed
land transportation, and after 1850, railroads were common in
Europe and North America. Unlike the canal, the railroad
could be built in areas deficient in water, and it was far less
sensitive to weather conditions. In addition, the railroad was
faster, by almost an order of magnitude, than any form of
transportation which preceeded it.

The railroad accompanied, some would argue instigated,
the industrial revolution. The new forms of manufacturing
which characterized the industrial revolution demanded large
quantities of raw materials and the shipment of great volumes
of products. The manufacturing enterprises were large in
scale, employing hundreds or even thousands of workers in a
single plant which occupied many hectares of land. Often the
plants were located in or near the cities with good
transportation, the larger urban places.

With manufacturing the cities grew, and their larger
populations demanded more food, more water, and more waste
removal. An important, if little discussed, transportation
improvement was for water movement. Until late in the
nineteenth century, most cities depended on nearby streams
for water supply, and such sewage removal as existed dumped
wastes back into those streams. The streams could not always
meet the increasing demands for water, and pollution
suggested a need for sewage removal (alas, not necessarily
treatment, just removal). Urban waterworks with thousands of
kilometers of aqueduct and distribution pipe were among the
most heroic of transportation projects. Water was brought to
New York City from the Catskill Mountains and to Los Angeles
from the Owens Valley and the Colorado River, hundreds of
kilometers away.

By 1900 the movement of goods to, from, and within cities
was no longer a constraint on growth of cities in North
America and Europe. The problem of goods transportation had
been resolved. In other parts of the world, the transportation systems remained primitive, but since 1900, there has
been a huge investment in the countries of Africa, Asia, and
Latin America (the poorer countries of which comprise the

Third World). Tens of thousands of kilometers of railroads and
hundreds of thousands of kilometers of road have been built
and improved. Roads have been especially important for, in
the twentieth century, trucks have become a major means for
moving goods. More costly to operate over long distances than
boats or trains, the truck makes up for its higher operating
costs with great flexibility and the ability to operate without
large investments in tracks or canals. In the twentieth
century, moving food and raw materials into cities and
removing urban products and wastes no longer constrains the
growth of cities anywhere in the world.

TRANSPORTATION AND URBAN GROWTH

In 1800 the typical Londoner ate little that was grown outside
the Thames Valley. In 1900 a middle-class London family was
likely to breakfast on bread made from American, Australian,
or Russian wheat, marmalade made from Spanish oranges,
bacon from Iowa or beef from Argentina, butter from Denmark
or even New Zealand, and tea from Ceylon or India sweetened
with sugar from Barbados. Only the milk at the breakfast
table was almost certain to have been produced in England.
The same improvements which made the diet possible made
larger urban populations possible.

The nineteenth century saw dramatic increases in both the
number and the population of cities, especially in North
America and Western Europe. In 1800 the United States had
only five cities with populations of 20,000 or more, and
Philadelphia, with about 50,000 residents, was the largest.
Indeed, Philadelphia was among the world's largest cities in
that year, though most of its population lived on a land area
of little more than two square kilometers. By 1900 Philadelphia
had dropped to second place among American cities, but its
population had climbed to over a million people spread across a
land area of several hundred square kilometers.

Land which had produced much of a city's fruits,
vegetables, and milk in 1800 had become sites for housing,
factories, and shops by 1900. In 1800 a walk of four or five
kilometers, about one hour, would take a person from one side
of London through its center to the opposite edge and into the
countryside. By 1900 a walk of that distance barely allowed a
pedestrian to reach the city's center from the closest point on
the edge (see fig. 1.1).

When even a short walk would take one all the way across
a city, most urban dwellers were within a few minutes walking
time of work, school, shops, churches, and other urban
activities. The walk was not always pleasant, for larger cities
were densely developed and congested. Streets were often so

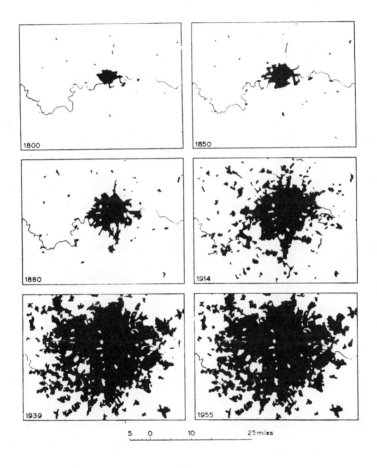

Fig. 1.1. The growth of London. Source: James H. Johnson, Urban Geography (New York: Pergamon Press, 2nd edition, 1972), p. 130.

narrow that two carts, or even two pack animals, could not pass. When crowded with shoppers and vehicles, it could be almost impossible to move forward along the major streets. In addition, the pedestrian had to watch for mud, dung left by pack animals, and slops thrown from the windows above. Given these conditions, people must have been glad that cities were small and distances were short.

With expansion of urban population and land area, distances were increased. Movement of people within the city became a primary transportation problem as distances increased beyond comfortable walks. Walking, the dominant form of transportation in older cities, was not feasible when cities spread over hundreds of square kilometers. There was a demand for faster ways to move people between their homes and various other places within cities.

TRANSPORTATION WITHIN THE CITY

When people must walk, they prefer to keep distances short, especially between places frequently visited. This is best accomplished by packing as much activity as possible into a small land area. If we must walk to the grocery store, we want a store within two or three blocks of home. More than that and the walk becomes too time consuming and lugging the packages home becomes too difficult. A grocery store must serve several hundred families to be successful. If no customer is to walk more than two blocks, then each of the blocks surrounding the store must house 40 to 50 families. A single large apartment building can house several times that many families, but most suburban areas in North America have 15 or fewer families per block.

The North American suburb is automobile oriented, and few of its residents are habitual pedestrians. Two key characteristics of pedestrian cities are high-intensity land use and mixed uses on adjacent land parcels. In the medieval city, where most people walked, streets were narrow and took up little land. Buildings were tall, and little space was left open for yards or other purposes. Building materials limited densities, as did transportation.

"Half the workmen . . . of the Strand . . . walked two miles to their work." This same Strand, a main thoroughfare which gives strangers an imposing idea of the wealth of London, may serve as an example of the packing together of human beings in that town. In one of its parishes, the Office of Health reckoned 581 persons per acre, although half the width of the Thames was reckoned in.(2)

- Karl Marx

Climbing four or five flights of stairs was the limit on vertical movement for most people. Given the limits on intensity, pedestrian cities still had population densities of 10,000 persons per square kilometer. The North American suburb rarely exceeds 5,000 persons in that space.

Within the pedestrian city, one is likely to find an intimate mixture of land uses, identified as functional integration. Modern Americans and many Europeans take the segregation of housing from workplaces and shopping for granted. A neighborhood is either residential or nonresidential, and nonresidential areas are further segregated into manufacturing, wholesaling, and retailing zones. In the pedestrian city, any block - and any single building - was likely to house people as well as provide space for manufacture, storage, and selling. The mixture would be illegal in most present-day cities of the United States. It violates zoning ordinances based on the "natural segregation" of incompatible activities.

This "natural segregation" is a product of improved urban transportation, which made it possible for workers to live away from their place of work. From the earliest days of cities, the rich had access to animals and wheeled vehicles, while almost everyone else walked. With transportation the rich could live in residential areas segregated from the noise, dirt, and odors which accompany manufacturing and retailing. The rest of the urban population was forced to live near, frequently in the same building as, the place where they were employed.

It was not until the middle of the nineteenth century that people other than the very rich could escape functionally integrated neighborhoods. The ability to live in one part of the city and work in another required cheap and fast passenger transportation. The railroad provided such transportation to a few people, though it was cheap only for those who were fairly wealthy. Train tickets were expensive, and the railroad was an inflexible type of transportation for use in cities. It could start and stop only at intervals of about two kilometers. The high cost and inflexibility of railroad transportation left a strong imprint on many cities. Fashionable suburbs were created along the railroad lines as the wealthier segments of society made use of the new transportation service.

> The [Paris] railways emanated from termini within the 1841 fortifications and were essentially designed to link the Capital with the Provinces. The suburbs thus followed the railways rather than the railways being planned to serve the suburbs.(3)
>
>   - Ian B. Thompson

The famed residential areas along the North Shore of Lake
Michigan near Chicago, the San Francisco Peninsula, and the
"Main Line" of Philadelphia all developed during the railroad
era.
      Because the trains stopped at stations two or more
kilometers apart, and most passengers walked from the stations
home, the railroad suburbs were separated from the central
city and from each other by tracts of land not yet urbanized.
On a map, the places looked rather like a string of pearls
graduated in size, with the smallest pearl at the outermost end
of the line (see fig. 1.2). Due to higher costs, fewer people
lived at the more distant stations. The pattern produced by
the railroad suburbs is one usually attributed to the automobile, <u>leapfrog sprawl</u> with patches of urban use mixed with
patches of agricultural land and other rural uses.

Fig. 1.2. "String of pearls" suburbs along a railroad line.

      At about the same time the railroad began to provide
transportation services for a few of the city's wealthiest
residents, horsecars and omnibuses were introduced in a
number of cities, beginning in Paris. Horsecar service was
flexible, if somewhat unreliable. Only a little money was
needed to lay tracks along existing streets, and stations were
not necessary as the cars could be started and stopped every
few meters. The costs for labor and animal energy were fairly
high, but they were low enough to allow middle-class people to
move into residential zones segregated from the noise, dirt,
and odors of commercial districts.

Horsecars were particularly subject to the vagaries of weather and biology. A heat wave, a cold snap, or an outbreak of an equine virus could halt service. An innovation which made city transportation both cheap and reliable was needed. The innovation came in the 1870s, when the cable car was introduced in the city still associated with that mode. The cable car was well suited to the hilly terrain of San Francisco, but that did not stop its use in the almost flat central area of Chicago. The cable car was the first mechanical transporation cheap enough to allow the working class to ride rather than walk to work and to shop. By 1885 many hundreds of kilometers of cable car lines had been laid along the streets of American cities, and for the first time in urban history, all but the poorest urban residents could afford to ride rather than walk.

More important than the cable car because it spread to many more cities was the electric trolley, tram, streetcar, or street railway, as it has been called in various places. Using electricity rather than a moving cable for motive power, the street railway was an inexpensive and rapid way of moving people from place to place within cities. While most people walk 4 to 6 kilometers per hour, a street railway can travel as fast as 50 kilometers per hour, though speeds of 20 kilometers per hour are more common. Energy costs per passenger-kilometer were modest, and fares could be kept low so that all but the least affluent could afford to use the street railway.

The effect of this new transportation was rapid and profound. Huge areas were prepared for residential development as people moved away from congested commercial districts. Because the new transportation mode was fast, there was less need for high-intensity development. Residential areas could allow larger amounts of space for recreation, and individual houses could be surrounded by open space. If a street railway was available for a shopping trip, then the trip could cover five or ten kilometers rather than five to ten blocks. The journey to work was lengthened from meters to kilometers, but the time spent in travel remained nearly constant for most passengers.

The residential development encouraged by the street railway is well illustrated in some of the older parts of Los Angeles. The sprawling and low-intensity urbanization of Los Angeles is usually attributed to the automobile, but it was present long before the automobile was more than just a rich person's toy. Los Angeles had one of the most extensive and best operated street railway systems in the United States. The quality of that system made it possible for people to work in central Los Angeles while living amid orange groves many kilometers away.

In spite of the high quality street railway system, Los Angeles was the first major city in which the automobile became the dominant form of transportation. The street railways were too restrictive to match the kind of life styles which Angelenos desired. The street railways converged on the Central Business District (CBD), and it was necessary to pass through that area even when one's destination was a considerable distance away in a different direction. A trip to the beach on a hot summer day took much longer by street railway than by automobile, and people soon choose the faster alternative.

The automobile has received much attention in the recent literature on transportation in cities. The private automobile has few defenders at present, though it is by far the most popular form of mechanical transportation ever introduced. It has a number of valuable characteristics which no other type of urban transportation has been able to duplicate. The automobile allows virtual door-to-door service, it allows great flexibility in the direction and the scheduling of trips, and it usually proves the fastest way of travelling between two places.

The disadvantages of the automobile are well known and frequently repeated. One disadvantage which is not so frequently recited is that the automobile does not work well in high-density environments. It requires a great deal of space per passenger carried, it demands much storage space when not in use, and it is inefficient when forced to stop and start frequently. In short, the automobile is poorly suited to the kinds of urban environments which worked well when walking, cable cars, and street railways were dominant.

On the other hand, the automobile is the only presently available form of transportation which works well in low-intensity environments such as the North American suburbs. Given a public desire for houses on large lots surrounded by open space, the automobile made suburban development a realistic proposition, opening to the middle class and even the poor a life style previously restricted just to the rich. The automobile is fast and flexible, and only a single passenger (the driver) is needed to justify a trip. People living in modern American suburbs are too thinly spread to make pedestrian movement feasible. There are not enough people within walking distance of stores, schools, and work-places. There are also too few people for effective and efficient public transit. Successful public transit demands many people with similiar points of origin and destination.

The dependence on automobiles is greatest in Australia, Canada, the United States, Sweden, and the other wealthy nations of Europe. Elsewhere, public transportation is still dominant, and in a few large cities many people still must walk. Public policy in some countries has tried to discourage automobile usage by prohibitions or restrictions on ownership or by limitations on where automobiles may be used. Other nations have attempted to encourage public transit usage through large subsidies. It has been estimated that each passenger on the Bay Area Rapid Transit (BART) in the San Francisco Bay Area is being subsidized to the amount of about $4 per trip. That payment from local, state, and federal tax revenues is in addition to the fare paid by the passenger. The subsidies in other cities and for other forms of transportation are even greater. Each dollar of subsidy is a dollar not available for other public uses, and in an era of concern about high taxes, one must thoroughly examine every subsidy. Do the benefits make the subsidy worthwhile?

In spite of the subsidization of BART, ridership has been far below expectations. The lack of passengers may have less to do with public stupidity in not using the rail systems than it has to do with the nature of urban land use in the San Francisco Bay Area. Like many other cities in the United States, the Bay Area has adapted to the automobile, and the car works well as the major means of urban transit. The city is so well adapted to the automobile that other transit modes do not work.

We can argue that the city is a product of its transportation system. In the next chapter we shall examine the relationship between land use and transportation in cities. We shall find that the urban land-use pattern is directly related to the transportation type which is dominant. Understanding the relationship is a key to understanding urban transportation problems and prospects.

2 Transportation and Land Use

LAND USED FOR TRANSPORTATION

Transportation is a major user of land in cities. In a typical North American city, about 5 percent of the total land area is used for port facilities, railroad yards and lines, pipelines and pumping stations, trucking terminals, and airports. Streets and highways use another 15 to 25 percent. Less land is used for streets and highways in older parts of cities than in newly developed suburban areas, and the amount varies depending on whether or not sidewalks, verges, and parking lots are included in the tabulation. An aerial photograph of central Chicago (fig. 2.1) provides striking evidence of transportation uses of urban land. A very large fraction of the land is used for streets and highways, another is devoted to water transportation, and most dramatically, huge blocks are railroad yards (not all of which are visible, since some have recently been covered by "air rights" buildings).

The importance of transportation for urban land use goes far beyond the use of land for transportation facilities. A careful examination of the photograph shows that most of the land near the port facilities and the railroad yards is occupied by large buildings of the types used for manufacturing, wholesaling, and warehousing. A generalized land-use map of central Chicago would make the connection between transportation terminals and those uses even clearer. Virtually all of the land near the transportation terminals is devoted to manufacturing, wholesaling, and warehousing. A land-use map from the mid 1920s, before trucks became important for moving goods, would show almost all of the manufacturing, wholesaling, and warehousing in Chicago concentrated in those locations. Since 1945 some of

Fig. 2.1. Aerial photograph of central Chicago.

the activities have been located elsewhere in the Chicago area,
but central Chicago, with its transportation terminals, remains
an important location.

Goods transportation is more visible and accounts for
much more land than passenger movement. Most passenger
routes operate on rights-of-way also used for transporting
goods. Cars and busses drive on the same highways used by
trucks, and passenger trains use tracks which also carry
freight trains. Some important passenger routes in Chicago
are below ground and not visible in the photograph, while the
city also has a famous elevated passenger railroad. In effect
it double-decks streets so that traffic flows at two levels.

In spite of its lower visibility, passenger transportation
has a strong impact on patterns of urban land use. Indeed, it
can be argued that it is the single most important determinant.
If we were to superimpose a map of the Chicago elevated and
subway lines on the photograph, the nature of the connection
between passenger transportation and land use would become
clearer. An area encircled by the elevated lines has given the
Chicago CBD its common name, "the Loop." Inside and
adjacent to the loop formed by the elevated lines, one finds
Chicago's major office district, retail shops, entertainment
facilities, and cultural amenities. Almost completely absent
from the Loop are manufacturing, wholesaling, and, most
notably, residences. Housing is the major user of land in
Chicago (and in most cities), yet only a tiny fraction of the
land in the Loop is used for housing. Much of that fraction is
devoted to hotels and other facilities for transients.

TRANSPORTATION AND RESIDENTIAL LAND USE

The elevated lines which form the Loop radiate outward away
from it. A kilometer or two away from the central area, they
pass into areas which are almost entirely residential. Housing
is by far the most important user of land, and small parcels in
other uses are usually for neighborhood services - small
stores, schools, churches, and similiar activities. Close to the
Loop, most residences are in high-density, multifamily
dwellings, as are many residences near major stations on the
elevated lines. With increasing distance outward, however,
the single-family detached house becomes dominant. Densities
of 5,000 or more families per square kilometer are common close
to the center, but in more distant residential areas, densities
fall below 2,000 families per square kilometer.

A careful observer making a field survey of housing in
Chicago is likely to discover that the greater the distance
away from the Loop, the younger the average age of dwelling
units. The decline in density and in age with increasing

distance from the CBD reflects both accessibility and demand. Before the automobile was a common possession of American families, only a few people were willing to spend the time and money commuting long distances. A total one-way journey from home to work of more than five kilometers was unusual in pedestrian cities, and most people lived much closer than that to their place of employment. When the street railway was introduced, time became a better measure of travel, and few people commuted more than 35 to 40 minutes one way from home to work. Those who walked still had trips of less than five kilometers, but street-railway passengers might travel as much as 15 or even 20 kilometers between home and work.

Some people, of course, were more willing and able to travel than others. Those with the most limited resources tended to remain closest to their employment, while people with great amounts of leisure and money sometimes chose to travel much further. Some of the rich, as we saw in Chapter 1, chose to move out from the congested part of the city early in urban history. They were able to move because they possessed private transportation or could afford high-priced public transportation. A few of the not-so-rich also chose to live at considerable distances outward, opting to spend a great share of their time and money on transportation. As a partial compensation for the expenditure, they found land to be much cheaper in the remoter parts of the city. Cheaper land allowed larger lots and houses surrounded by open space, the type of low-density environment which we today associate with suburbs.

The automobile allowed even faster urban travel, and in a 35-to-40-minute trip, automobile drivers and passengers could go 25 kilometers more. Since the automobile did not require large investments in tracks and stations but could use existing roads and streets, it offered great directional flexibility. Land considered inaccessible because of distance to employment zones or to public transit stops was opened to development by the automobile. The automobile increased the radius of the city and thus exponentially increased the amount of land available for urban development. Its directional flexibility allowed use of land in the wedges between the radial public transit corridors.

PATTERNS OF URBAN LAND USE

The spatial pattern of urban growth (see fig. 2.2) can be visualized as beginning with a small compact core, the pedestrian city. When street railways were built, they radiated outward from the core and gave the city a star shape. Along the lines, urbanization might extend outward more than

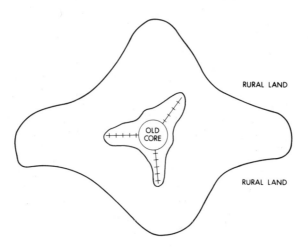

Fig. 2.2 Urban growth eras. Expected distortions from concentric growth patterns based on street railways (inner line) and automobiles (outer limit) lead to an overall star shape for the city. Source: Adapted from John S. Adams, "Residential Structure of Midwestern Cities," Annals of the Association of American Geographers 60 (1970):56.

ten kilometers, but in between the lines, the radius was not much more than five kilometers maximum walking distance. The automobile allowed the city to again become compact, that is circular, but on a very much larger scale. The radius was extended to more than 20 kilometers from the core in all directions (except, of course, over water).

The pattern is reflected in the density, age, and use of structures. The old pedestrian city is now mainly devoted to retail selling, offices, and factories. The mixture of functions that characterized the pedestrian era has been replaced by a functional segregation as the pedestrian city, or much of it, has become the CBD. Along the radial rail lines, most land is devoted to housing, often at high density in the form of apartments and row houses. Away from the radial lines and toward the outer edges of the city, one finds the single-family detatched houses characterized in the United States as suburban. These are the most recent additions to the city, and the result is an age pattern similar to the growth rings of a tree. The oldest structures are near the center, and the newest are near the outer edge.

The newest areas are almost entirely dependent on the automobile, and large quantities of land within them are devoted to its use and storage. The areas are too remote for walking and too low-density for good public transportation. In these areas at the edge, the automobile works well, but workers commuting toward the older urban core find congestion to be a problem. The trip is slow as too many vehicles attempt to use roads and streets built prior to the automobile age, and the lack of CBD parking leads to high prices and short tempers.

Increasing numbers of workers and shoppers are finding the trip to the CBD unnecessary. In the late 1930s, and especially in the decade from 1950 to 1960, retailers discovered that they could profitably locate large stores outside the CBD. In the regional shopping center, they recreated many features of the CBD with the added feature of ample and free parking. Located along major streets in areas toward the edge of the city, the centers attracted shoppers who drove. The success of the shopping centers was immediate. As increasing numbers of regional shopping centers were built, the CBDs of many North American cities all but lost their retail function. Taking a cue from retailers, after 1960 many offices moved to suburban office parks, while manufacturers located new plants near express highways at the edge of the city.

Express highways have become a major determinant of retail, office, and factory location. Limited access highways, known as Interstate Highways in the United States, motorways in Britain, and autobahns in Germany, have been built to and through most major cities. High speed and great capacity, attained mainly through limits on the number of entry and exit points, allow use by ever increasing numbers of both passenger and goods vehicles. Intersections of two express highways have proven most attractive locations for shops and for employment centers. The intersections of circumferential highways (beltways or orbitals) with radial routes leading out from the CBD have been especially important. Concentration of economic activities at these nodes creates a series of CBD-like centers in most American metropolitan areas.

Many of the new centers are outside the incorporated political jurisdiction in which the CBD is located. The political jurisdiction of Chicago includes just a part of Cook County, Illinois. The urbanized area centering on the Loop includes all of that county plus parts of five other counties in Illinois, two counties in Indiana, and two counties in Wisconsin. Altogether there are several hundred units of local government, and using a political definition of Chicago as just the incorporated city would be far too narrow for our purposes. In this book, a functional definition is used, viewing the city as the whole area linked by housing opportunities, jobs, shopping facilities, and cultural amenities. Commuting patterns are a major means of identifying the functional unit. Using a functional definition of Chicago based on commuting patterns, shopping patterns, and the use of cultural amenities, Chicago includes about 7 million people rather than the 2 million who live in the politically incorporated city.

Adoption of such a functional definition is essential if we are to understand urban transportation and its connection to urban land use. Except for Berlin, political boundaries of cities rarely have much influence on transportation, or on land use for that matter. There is even movement across international boundaries in metropolitan areas, as for example the United States-Canadian border in the Detroit urban area. While political boundaries have only a small impact on movement patterns, however, political conflicts can make resolution of urban transportation and land-use problems very difficult. Failure to understand the relationships between land use and transportation in cities has resulted in creation of many of those problems.

MODELS OF URBAN LAND USE

The land-use pattern we described in Chicago could be found, with differences of detail, in most large North American cities. Chicago was selected because it has been a major laboratory for economists, geographers, and sociologists studying urban land use.

> In the early part of this century Chicago was the centre of a remarkable, almost frantic, outburst of interest in the city.(1)
>
>   B.T. Robson

From studies of Chicago and many other cities, these social scientists have developed generalized statements or models of urban land use. Like all models, these general statements are not exactly descriptive of any particular case. Instead, they are intended to show the similarities of organization which characterize all cities. Urban land-use models provide a tool for analysis, for breaking the complex whole into parts and examining how the parts relate to each other. For that reason it is useful to introduce simplified versions of some urban land-use models before dealing further with urban transportation patterns and problems.

The oldest and most important of the models was developed in Chicago in the 1920s and has been greatly elaborated since. It is usually called the concentric-zone or concentric-ring model. Its origins were in observations similiar to those made about Chicago earlier in this chapter: 1) the central portion of the city where major long-distance transportation lines converge (the Loop in Chicago) is almost totally nonresidential but contains much of the city's employment, retailing, and cultural activities (the housing it does contain is primarily for transients); 2) there is an age gradient, with the earliest areas of development in and near the CBD and the most recent development at the outer edge; 3) in residential areas, there is a density gradient, with large numbers of people per square kilometer close to the CBD and much smaller numbers at the outer edge of the city; 4) in addition, it was noted that there is a social-class gradient - low income people, often members of minority linguistic or racial groups, live close to the CBD in higher density, older residential areas; as one travels further outward, the incomes of residents rise, while the proportion of minority group members falls.

> The upper classes enjoy healthy country air and live in luxurious and comfortable dwellings which are linked to the centre of Manchester by omnibusses which run every fifteen or thirty minutes. To such an extent has the convenience of the rich been considered in the planning of Manchester that these plutocrats can travel from their houses to their places of business in the centre of the town by the shortest routes. . ., without realizing how close they are to the misery and filth which lie on both sides of the road.(2)
>
>   Frederich Engels

The concentric-zone model (see fig. 2.3) generalizes from these observations to state that the city is organized into a series of concentric zones or rings surrounding the CBD. The model as originally developed had little to say about the organization of nonresidential land uses except to note their concentration in the CBD. The model was primarily concerned with differences in residential use and stated that each zone was characterized by people of a particular social status. As elaborated, the relationship between social status and residential location was explained by the interaction of accessibility and demand for land. The most accessible land was desired because of its proximity to employment and other activities of the CBD. Living there one could minimize the time and money spent on transportation.

Geometry is important here, especially the formula for the area of a circle, $A = \pi r$.(3) It tells us that there is a geometric increase in the area of a circle with an arithmetic increase in radius. There is not much land within 1 kilometer of the CBD, within a short walking distance. Thus, while

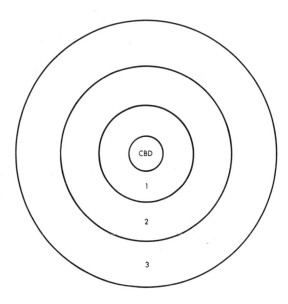

Fig. 2.3. The concentric-zone model. Ring 1 housing for low income people; ring 2 housing for middle income people; ring 3 housing for rich people. Source: Adapted from Robert E. Park and Ernest W. Burgess, The City (Chicago: The University of Chicago Press, 1925), p. 51.

many people demand land close to the CBD, there is not much land available to be divided among them. In societies where price is a function of demand, many people competing for a small amount of land leads to high land prices. As the price rises, people "economize" in their use of land, or in the terminology usually applied, they use the land at high intensity, crowding much activity into small parcels.

High-intensity land uses are accompanied by noise, odors, dirt, and frequent contacts between strangers. To some people, these are of no concequence, and other people have no way of avoiding them. In the English speaking world, people generally prefer to live in areas where land-use intensity is lower and the problems of noise and the like less intense. They are willing to trade accessibility for space, to spend more time and money on travel in order to escape the urban core. The geometric increase in the amount of land available makes it possible to obtain ever larger parcels of land for a given budget as distance away from the core increases. Since some activities cannot successfully locate outside the CBD, there is also less competition, which further lowers the price.

The result is a land-price gradient with highest land prices in the CBD and a sharp fall in prices as distance increases away from it.

To use the lower-cost land, however, people must be willing and able to spend more time and money on travel. The poor may have a surplus of time, but they lack money. Walking or the cheapest forms of public transit are all they can afford, so they require residences within a short distance of employment opportunities and necessary services. In practice the poor are concentrated close to the CBD where low transportation costs combine with the availability of old, often decrepit, and therefore fairly inexpensive housing. The low cost of the housing is deceptive, for the amount of space per person is small; that is to say, intensity of use is high.

The concentric-zone model is based on a competition for space decided in terms of ability and willingness to pay for transportation. There is an incentive to live close to the CBD, low transportation costs, but that advantage is countered by the problems of high intensity. The attractiveness of low-intensity areas is, in turn, reduced by transportation costs. Ability to pay those costs is an important factor deciding which income group lives at a given distance away from the CBD. The result is an income gradient with poorer people close to the CBD and richer people near the outer edge of the city. Willingness to pay also plays a role. Transportation costs time as well as money. Some of the rich choose to live in high-intensity residential areas near the CBD for they are unwilling to spend time on travel. With money the disadvantages can be mitigated (soundproofing and air-conditioning, for example).

The original concentric-zone model did not deal with the concentration of some rich people near the CBD. That, among other problems, prompted development of alternative models of urban land use including the sector model. Its details need not detain us, but it does look at the role of transportation in a slightly different way. The concentric-zone model assumes an isotropic transportation surface. The cost of transportation on an isotropic surface is solely a function of distance. A trip of five kilometers costs the same amount of time and money (and energy) no matter what the direction of travel. In the real world, transportation costs vary with direction as well as distance; the surface is anisotropic. As an example, it is faster and usually cheaper to travel five kilometers on an express highway than to go the same distance on traffic-light-ridden streets parallel to it.

The sector model implicitly assumes anisotropic transportation. Radial routes leading out of the CBD are assumed to be better than other routes within the city. It also assumes an income segregation in the use of transportation. Commuter railroads were the domain of the rich when they were important carriers of commuters. In many American cities at present, buses are almost exclusively used by the poor. The first mechanical transportation routes generally served the rich, pulling them out of the central area to houses near the lines. This created the initial sector, an area of wealth (see fig. 2.4). As more routes were added, radiating in different directions from the CBD, they served less affluent people, each new line tending to serve lower income people than the lines which came before it. On a map, the resulting pattern of income in residential areas looks like a pie sliced into wedges.

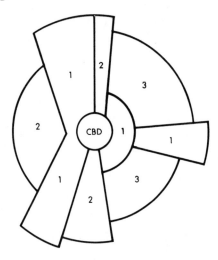

Fig. 2.4. The sector model. Areas numbered 1 lower income residential; areas numbered 2 high income residential; areas numbered 3 medium income residential. Source: Adapted from Chauncy D. Harris and Edward L. Ullman, "The Nature of Cities," Annals of the American Academy of Political and Social Science 242 (1945):13.

Neither the concentric-zone nor the sector model says much about the location of urban activities other than housing. They both assume that the CBD is the locus of most economic activity. In the 1920s and 1930s, when the two models were originally developed, that assumption was justified. In all but a handful of cities there was an area like Chicago's Loop, where employment and nonresidential land uses were concentrated.

Since 1945 the dominance of the CBD has declined. Already in 1930, Los Angeles showed the future form of cities with employment and other traffic generating activites scattered into several different centers. To assume a single dominant core and deduce residential land-use patterns on the basis of concentric-zone or sector models is not appropriate in Los Angeles, a multicentric city. Families choose residences not on the basis of transportation to the CBD, but rather on access to the particular center or centers where members work, shop, seek services, or are entertained.

The multiple-nuclei model (see figure 2.5) is an effort to generalize about land-use patterns in cities like Los Angeles. It is becoming increasingly important as more and more centers

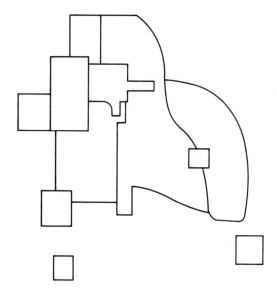

Fig. 2.5. The multiple nuclei model. A schematic diagram of land use zones in a city with several employment centers. Source: Adapted from Chauncy D. Harris and Edward L. Ullman, "The Nature of Cities," Annals of the American Academy of Political and Social Science 242 (1945):13.

of economic activity appear outside CBDs. There are at least two types of multicentricity. Los Angeles is an example of a city without a dominant center. No one center contains markedly more activity than any of several others. Thus the Los Angeles CBD is not much more important as an employment center than each of several other nuclei (Westwood, Wilshire Boulevard, Hollywood, and Beverly Hills, to name several). It is less important as a retail selling area than some of the others.

Chicago at present illustrates the second type of multicentricity. It has a dominant center which is encircled by a series of subdominant clusters of economic activity. The Loop still contains hundreds of thousands of jobs, the largest stores, and most of the city's major civic and cultural facilities. In spite of that, large employment concentrations, major shopping facilities, and increasing amounts of civic and cultural activity can be found at other centers within the metropolitan area. None of the other centers comes close to matching the size and importance of the Loop, but together the subdominant centers contain a large fraction of Chicago's economic cultural life.

The multiple-nuclei model says little about the organization of residential land use in respect to the various centers. Application of the transportation relationships which influence residential patterns in the concentric-zone and sector models leads to a most complicated overall pattern. The journey to work remains a major consideration for people in multiple-nuclei cities, and residences will be selected on the basis of transportation and land costs. The scatter of employment, and the lowering of central area land-use intensity, leads to more even overall distribution of land-use intensity and a more even distribution of land prices. Ideally housing for all social and income groups should be available near each of the centers, but as we shall see later, that is not usually the case.

The concentric-zone and sector models best describe cities where rail transportation is dominant. The multiple-nuclei model is most appropriate for cities dependent on the automobile. In the 1920s, Chicago, dominated by the Loop, was dependent on commuter railroads, elevated lines, and street railways. Today some of those lines still bring workers to the Loop, but Chicago, like most American cities, is primarily dependent on automobiles for passenger transportation. Trips to outlying centers, and many trips to the Loop, are by automobile.

At this point one might reasonably object that the models are biased toward United States cities. What about cities in Europe and the Third World? As we shall see, the American models fit European cities rather well. Like North America, Europe has long been dependent on mechanical transportation for passenger movement in cities. Of course European cities had a much longer pedestrian history, and they have had a shorter automobile-dominated period, but in the main, their land-use patterns have evolved in a manner similar to the American experience.

The Third World is a different matter. Public transportation is limited and automobile ownership very limited, so many Third World urban residents are still pedestrians, walking to work, to shop, and to obtain services. As we saw

in Chapter 1, there is a tendency toward functional integration
in pedestrian cities. Jobs and residents are mixed together in
neighborhoods where richer and poorer people also mingle. As
in pedestrian cities of Europe prior to 1850, the very rich and
the abject poor live apart from the mass.

The pattern of land use is almost the reverse of that
proposed by the concentric-zone model. The very rich cluster
near the center, while the poorest are pushed to the outer
edge of the city. Many Third World cities are not industrial
and commercial centers but rather political and administrative
places. Their central areas are pleasant, with large parks,
elegant squares, and fancy gardens surrounded by housing for
the rich. Such polluting industry as the cities contain is
pushed to the outer suburbs where the poor reside.

Many Third World cities are similar in land use to Paris
just before the French Revolution. The aristocracy and the
rich lived near the center, while the poor, many of whom
worked in the households of the rich, were forced to walk
from suburb to central city. In pre-Revolution Paris,
distances were short. From the poor areas of Faubourg
(suburb) St. Denis to the elegant precincts near the Tuileries
was less than five kilometers. In contemporary Caracas,
Lagos, and Bangkok, the distance from squatter settlements in
the suburbs to jobs in the central city can be upwards of 20
kilometers. The historical pattern is the same, but the scale
of the Third World city in the late twentieth century is very
much greater.

CHANGING LAND USE AND TRANSPORTATION

Urban land-use patterns are dynamic. A land-use map drawn
at the beginning of a decade is likely to be badly out of date
ten years later. During the decade, new land at the edge of
the city is urbanized, while some older areas near the core
may be abandoned and no longer utilized. Examples of
abandonment can be found in derelict manufacturing areas near
railroad yards. Land devoted to one use the year the map is
compiled may be used for a very different purpose ten years
later.

Urban land-use models are powerful tools for analysis and
explanation of changes. They require us to consider factors
which cause land uses to change. The growth of the urban
population and the consequent need for greater amounts of
land has been a major sources of land-use change. The
models lead us to expect outward expansion of the city away
from the CBD as population grows. In the expansion, areas
once used for housing are converted to sites for factories,
offices, and shops; housing is passed from higher to lower

income people; and new sites are created for housing on once
rural land. The models discussed above do not deal directly
with forces of change such as new technology and changing
life styles. We know, however, that technological
developments, particularly in manufacturing and construction,
play a most important role. Likewise, changed life styles, as
for example the present trend toward one- and two-person
families, have strong impacts. Smaller families mean more
dwellings are needed to house a given number of people.

Transportation remains the key to understanding land-use
change. It defines the possibilities for change. There is a
limit on the time and money people can spend on
transportation, especially on travel to and from work.
The faster and cheaper transportation is made, the greater are
the alternatives when locating housing, jobs, and services. In
a city with inadequate mechanical transportation, it is not
feasible to locate housing for workers more than six to ten
kilometers from workplaces. This has been shown in Third
World nations where new housing estates are inadequately
served by public transportation. Beyond reasonable walking
distance of employment centers, some of the estates are underutilized, even in cities with severe housing shortages.

A dramatic land-use change in the United States city has
been the decline of the CBD as a retail selling area. Most
cities have experienced shop closures, and in some smaller
cities, the CBD has nearly lost its retail function. Expensive
improvements, including pedestrian malls and large parking
lots, have failed to attract new shops or even to keep existing
stores. People prefer to drive automobiles to regional
shopping centers, avoiding the congestion and parking
problems common in the CBD. With too few shoppers, stores
either close or move from the CBD to more accessible locations.

Changes for goods transportation have also caused
land-use change, as shown in the derelict industrial buildings
near ports and railroad yards. Attempts to attract new
manufacturers have largely failed. Well served by old
transportation modes, the old manufacturing areas are not well
suited to trucks. They are too high-intensity and too far
from good highways. In addition they lack adequate space for
workers to park.

Manufacturers and retailers have favored locations close
to major highways at or just beyond the edge of the city.
Construction of a freeway near the center of a city can result
in land-use change as businesses and families are displaced, a
change which has received much attention. In suburban
areas, the effects of a new freeway can lead to a flury of
construction near proposed interchanges, converting land from
rural to urban uses. Clusters of high-intensity development
surrounded by still rural land can result, a land-use pattern sometimes called leapfrog sprawl. It is rare that the

surrounding land remains rural for long, however. Soon much of it is covered by single-family detatched houses.

The easily demonstrated connection between highway construction and land-use change has led some authorities to conclude that new transportation facilities of any type can be used to mold land-use patterns. The new transportation must be superior to modes already in use: it must be faster, more direct, or substantially cheaper for the users. Since 1945 most urban transportation investment in the United States has been directed to roads and highways. Improved facilities for automobile transportation have diverted users from public transit, especially from rail lines. It has been argued that improvements to rail transit can bring riders back, and that high-quality, new, rail rapid transit systems can capture some of the traffic now using automobiles for travel in the city.

BART in San Francisco and Metro in Washington, D.C. have been designed to increase the speed of travel between the CBDs and residential areas in the two cities. The improvement is intended to reduce automobile traffic and, not incidentally, to maintain activity in the CBDs. Rail rapid transit, under optimal conditions, is expensive to build but cheap to operate on a passenger-kilometer basis. A large investment in tracks, stations, and vehicles is necessary before any service can begin. Once in service, and utilized close to capacity, rail transit is energy efficient - using little energy per passenger-kilometer - and labor efficient. To be efficient, the rail system must carry many passangers on each trip.

The cost of building lines and the need to carry many passengers lead to convergence of the rail lines at a single center. That center is then the most accessible place on the system and location nearby should be attractive to activities which require large numbers of workers or shoppers. When a new system is designed, its central point is likely to be placed where large numbers of people already shop or work. BART's point of maximum access is in the office district of the Oakland CBD, while the most accessible point for Washington's Metro is the basement of its largest department store. In both cities, it is hoped that use of the rail lines will halt or reverse the movement of jobs and shops from the CBDs.

Unlike rail rapid transit systems, road vehicles do not require much initial investment for rights-of-way. Freeways can cost hundreds of millions of dollars, but vehicles can operate on poorly graded dirt tracks. Most cities had a system of streets suitable for automobiles and trucks long before the internal combustion engine was invented. Road vehicles are expensive to operate, especially in high-intensity environments. At full load, an automobile uses far more energy per passenger-kilometer than a fully loaded train. On the other hand, an automobile is almost as energy efficient

with on passenger as it is with a full load. A train with only
a few passengers uses much more energy per passenger-
kilometer than would be used if those passengers were moved
by car.

The energy consumption advantages of the automobile in
low intensity environments combine with its advantage of
directional flexibility. The ability to operate on many different
types of surface means automobiles can be driven over
numerous routes to provide door-to-door service, except in
high-intensity environments where parking is a problem.
Door-to-door service is convenient, and it often means faster
travel. These advantages have not escaped the notice of
urbanites, as evidenced by the rapid spread of automobile
ownership and use even where public transit is excellent.

The rapid spread of the automobile has been accompanied
by even more rapid land-use change. Growing urban
populations, increasing consumer incomes, technological
advances, and altered life styles have combined to generate
new land-use patterns. The chief differences between land
use in automobile cities and in rail cities are patterns of
land-use intensity and functional segregation. Rail transit is
best suited to a CBD-dominated city where land-use intensity
is high and there is a rigid segregation of functions. As the
automobile comes to dominate, intensity and the degree of
functional segregation decline.

The difference between automobile and rail cities raises a
most important question concerning current land use and
transportation goals in the cities of Europe and North America.
Can a city be organized successfully to split transportation
between the two modes? A number of years ago, a major
American manufacturing firm introduced the advertising slogan
"balanced transportation" (not suprisingly the firm
manufactures both rail and road transportation equipment).
The phrase became popular among civic officials as they
promoted schemes such as BART and Metro. The officials
have assumed that cities can be organized to accept both rail
rapid transit and automobile transportation. As we shall see,
that is not a safe assumption.

3 Urban Transportation in Wealthy Nations

THE USE AND THE COSTS OF TRANSPORTATION

No urban resident needs to be reminded of the problems associated with the automobile in cities - safety, air pollution, and visual blight getting the most attention. In the past few years city dwellers have also become aware of public transit problems. There has been a vicious circle of declining ridership leading to higher fares leading to further declines in ridership. In the United States, huge deficits have driven private operators close to bankruptcy. To maintain at least some service, local governments have taken ownership of the lines and then provided large subsidies from tax revenues.

The automobile is blamed for the problems of public transit. There is a correlation between decline in usage of public transit and increase in automobile usage. The decline began as early as 1920 in some American cities, and it is now rapid in European cities. It seems that as families acquire automobiles, they are not inclined to use buses, trains, or other public transit when going to visit friends, to shop or to work.

The journey to work, commuting, is the most important type of passenger transportation in cities. The journey to work accounts for a plurality of all trips made in cities as workers travel from home to employment and return. The pattern of commuting trips is regular in time and space. Most workers commute on a fixed schedule over a specific route, travelling at the same times each workday, using the same roads or public transit lines.

Accurate predictions of demand for transportation to and from workplaces can be made knowing little more than the number of workers, the shift schedules, and the location of

31

housing. The typical time pattern has two demand peaks - the
morning and afternoon rush hours - and a demand trough in
the early morning hours when few people are commuting to or
from work (see fig. 3.1). The type of employment which is

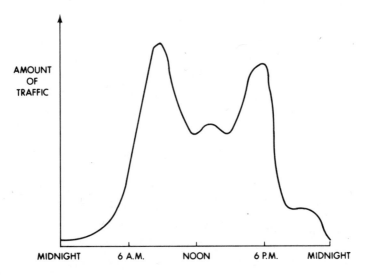

Fig. 3.1 A typical time pattern of traffic to and from workplaces.

dominant in a city determines the exact times of the peaks as
well as the level of peak demand. Cities like Washington,
D.C., where office employment is dominant, concentrate
demand into rush hours. Office jobs typically begin between 8
and 9 A.M., and the workday ends between 4:30 and 6 P.M.
Most commuting is thus concentrated into the hours between 7
and 9 A.M. and 4:30 and 7 P.M. A number of manufacturing
plants operate 24 hours each day, and shifts begin at various
times during the day. Industrial cities such as Pittsburgh
have a somewhat more even spread of travel demand through
the day.
      Time   variations   in   travel   demand   are   important
determinants of transportation service, especially for public
transit. At the lowest levels of demand in the early morning
hours, there may not be enough potential passengers to justify
any service, while congestion during rush hours may deter
potential passengers. The ideal pattern of use spreads
demand evenly through the day. When demand is unevenly
spread, it becomes difficult to operate public transit
efficiently. If there are enough vehicles to meet rush-hour
demand, then there are too many vehicles the remainder of the

day. Similarly, if a highway is designed and built to carry peak-hour traffic, then its capacity will be excessive the rest of the time.

Adequate rush-hour transportation requires expensive equipment and facilities which are idle much of the day, but inadequate transportation facilities mean congestion. If, for example, a highway is inadequate for peak-hour demand, then it is overused during that period. Overcrowding a highway means increased travel times, safety hazards, and pollutant emissions. Inadequate rush-hour service on public transit leads potential passengers to other modes, such as driving to work instead of riding the bus. It may lead employers to relocate at sites where congestion is not a problem. New suburban offices and factories minimize congestion problems but require workers to use automobiles for commuting.

Commuting is only one type of transportation demand. People also travel to shop, for social purposes (to visit friends and relatives), for recreation, and between different workplaces. These demands are more irregular in time than the journey to work. Social and recreational travel are especially difficult to anticipate, but fortunately they have peak demand periods when demand for commuter travel is low - on weekends, holidays, and in the late evening. Trips between workplaces help to level demand through the business day, since they primarily occur between the morning and evening rush hours.

The journey to shop, the second most frequent type of urban travel, presents the greatest problems. It varies in importance from season to season and from day to day during the week. Since shopping hours are roughly the same as employee shift hours, demand for trips to shop adds to peak-hour commuter demand, though shopping trips are more evenly spread through the day then are commuter journeys. Long opening hours in the United States further diffuse the demand as shopping is done in the evening. In Europe, where late opening is unusual and many stores close at weekends, the shopping-trip increment to rush-hour traffic is substantial.

The trip to shop is, on the average, shorter than the trip to work. Many shopping trips are to the neighborhood grocery market, while others are to nearby shopping centers. Trips to the CBD are reserved for occasions when expensive or unusual items are on the shopping list. Trips to nearby shopping areas may be pedestrian, but for longer trips, such as those to the CBD, public transit is less favored than the automobile. It is easier to carry large and bulky packages in an automobile than on a crowded bus or train.

Transportation geographers talk of desire lines, connections between origins and destinations. For a shopper wishing to purchase groceries, a desire line would connect home, the point of origin, and the grocery store, the destination. Drawn on a map, the desire lines for urban residents show the frequency of potential trips in various directions. In a city with a dominant CBD, many of the desire lines coincide or nearly coincide, and on a map the resultant pattern looks like a multirayed star (see fig. 3.2a). In multiple-nuclei cities with jobs, shopping centers, and public services clustered in several locations, the mapped pattern is a complex web (see fig 3.2b). In the city with a dominant CBD, many of the desire lines nearly coincide, while in the multiple-nuclei city few of them coincide.

The greater the coincidence of desire lines, the more feasible is public transit. To be financially viable, public transit must carry a large number of passengers from similar points of origin to similiar destinations. In a city with a dominant CBD, many workers and shoppers have similar origins and destinations. An extreme example of such a city is Moscow in the USSR. About half of the Soviet capital's jobs and most of its major stores are in the central area. Local authorities estimate that at least 30 percent of Moscow's 8 million residents travel to and from its CBD each workday. By contrast, fewer than 15 percent of the New York metropolitan area population travel into Manhattan each day.

The great flow of people to and from a concentrated area makes it worthwhile to provide fast and frequent public transit. Mosow's subways are known for their opulence. They should also be recognized for the huge numbers of passengers carried and for the high frequency of trains. Most cars run full, and trains are rarely more than five minutes apart. In addition to the Metro, buses, electric buses (trackless trolleys), and street railways converge on the center and on outlying stations of the radial subway system. On a map, the pattern of public transit lines looks like the root system of a tree, with the roots converging at the base, the CBD.

Moscow has a circumferential superhighway, but to this date, it has had a small impact on commuter travel. The absence of suburban workplaces, and more importantly the lack of private automobiles make highways unimportant for commuter travel. Ownership of an automobile is a limited privilege, but the number of automobiles in Moscow is rapidly growing. At the same time, the Soviet government has adopted a policy of decentralization. New factories and offices are being located outside the central area, usually in clusters called new towns.

Moscow's official development goals are similar to those of another authoritarian capital, Stockholm. Decentralization is more advanced in the wealthy Scandinavian city, where most families own automobiles. Decentralizing employment and constructing express highways, Swedish planners have encouraged automobile commuting. The multiple-nuclei city which is evolving means that desire lines for travel coincide

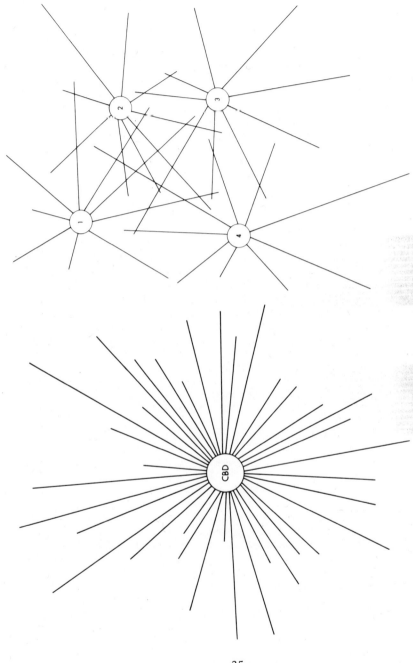

Fig. 3.2a Travel desire lines in a city Fig. 3.2b Travel desire lines in a multiple nuclei city. with a dominant CBD.

ever less frequently, reducing the potential for successful public transit. Too few people wish to make the same trip at the same time to fill more than a part of the seats on a bus.

In spite of this, the Swedish planners have had a rail rapid transit system blasted through the hard granite under Stockholm. This expensive facility has been justified as a necessary connection between satellite employment centers and the CBD. Until recently there has been little official recognition of the contradiction between transportation development and land-use goals. If decentralization is to reduce the density of employment in the CBD, it also reduces demand for transportation to and from that zone. Conversely, construction of rail rapid transit lines converging on the center and capable of carrying tens of thousands of passengers each hour encourages the location of high-intensity activities in the CBD.

Since passengers have some choice, even in Sweden, the rail system is proving much less attractive than the planners anticipated. The lines carry fewer passengers than their capacity allows, making the cost per passenger-kilometer far higher than expected. People are opting to use automobiles when going to work, and especially when going to shop, to visit friends, and between workplaces. The greater flexibility of the automobile is favored, even though the cost of its use is sometimes greater in cash. In addition, many of the satellite employment centers have been designed to allow workers and shoppers to walk from home.

When filled to capacity, rail rapid transit vehicles can operate at a low cost per passenger-kilometer. In the United States the cost can be as low as 0.5¢ per passenger-kilometer. When carrying a full load of five or six passengers, the cost per passenger-kilometer for an automobile is at least 5¢ and can be much higher. Few automobiles used for commuting or shopping trips carry a full passenger load, and the car with only a single passenger - the driver - is common. That raises the cost per passenger-kilometer to at least 20¢. When travelling with only a few passengers, the rail rapid transit cost may rise to several dollars per passenger-kilometer. The labor, energy, and capital requirements are nearly identical whether the train travels empty or crammed with standing passengers.

The difference in cost between empty and full vehicles is less for buses than trains, but a nearly empty bus costs far more per passenger-kilometer than does an automobile with only a driver. To be justified, public transit must carry large numbers of passengers, for only then can the advantages of low costs per passenger be realized. Large numbers of passengers are likely to use public transit only when the desire lines for travel of many people coincide or nearly coincide. If only a few desire lines coincide, public transit

fares must be high to cover costs, or large subsidies must be
provided.

SUBSIDIES AND PUBLIC TRANSIT

Early urban transportation companies were private,
profit-making enterprises. The profits, often agumented by
returns from land-development schemes, could be substantial.
To encourage use of lines, the transportation companies
promoted residential development in more remote locations along
the routes. In the United States, however, profits began to
fall after 1920, and by 1950, losses were common. To maintain
public transit service, local governments acquired the
companies. What had been a profitable business became a
"necessary public utility," a service to be continued even
when subsidies were necessary.
    Reduced demand for public transit reduced farebox
revenue. On more than a few lines, revenues raised at the
farebox have not been adequate to pay for the necessary
capital, labor, and energy, and only a subsidy has allowed
continued operation. Subsidy means that those who use and
benefit from the service do not pay its entire cost. The poor,
the young, the handicapped, and the elderly are dependent on
public transit. Subsidy for their benefit is politically popular.
    Subsidy is not needed for all public transit service.
Certain services remain profitable. Privately owned taxis
return profits to their owners while providing much service,
albeit at a high cost per passenger-kilometer. Among bus and
rail lines in public ownership, some carry so many passengers
that farebox revenues more than cover capital, labor, and
energy costs. Some of that excess is used to subsidize lines
where revenues are less than costs, but increasing amounts of
subsidy come from tax revenues.
    Determining who is being subsidized is a most complicated
task. The way fares are collected is important. American
cities often charge a flat fare, and passengers pay the same
amount no matter how far they travel. English cities have
distance-based fares with the charge increasing as the distance
travelled increases. In Germany some cities have an honor
system with no regular check on fare payment and only
occasional spot checks to catch passengers who have not
purchased tickets. Most public transit systems offer reduced
fares or free travel to school children, the handicapped, and
"senior citizens." Within the various types of fare collection
there are great differences in the amount charged per
kilometer travelled. In United States cities, it varies from a
fraction of a cent to over 50 cents.

It would seem that the higher the fare paid by a
passenger, the lower the subsidy would be. Reality is not
that simple. High fares may reflect limited usage of a line.
While a passenger pays a high fare, the cost of providing the
service still exceeds the revenue. Conversely a low fare
charged on a heavily used line may still return a profit.
Likewise, distance is not always as significant as it appears.
It may cost little more to carry one passenger ten kilometers
than it costs to transport another only 5 kilometers. This is
especially true when capital costs, rather than labor or energy
costs, are dominant.

In the face of these complexities, it is still possible to
determine where some subsidies are spent. As the number of
passengers carried increases, the subsidy per passenger
declines. It is expensive to build rail lines and operate buses
in high-intensity areas. Land is costly and congestion is a
problem. In spite of the higher costs, revenues in
high-intensity areas are likely to match or exceed them.
Density translates into demand and makes operation of full
vehicles more probable. The difficulties of driving automobiles
in high-density environments encourage public transit usage
and increase the possibility of break-even or profitable
operation.

Areas of low land-use intensity generate little revenue
per square kilometer. The smaller number of people means
lower demand and thus justification for fewer services. Low
frequency of service is inconvenient. Passengers must wait or
walk long distances to catch a bus or train. The automobile is
more convenient, and in low-intensity areas, its use is easy.
Automobile use reduces passenger loads on public transit, and
the smaller loads mean higher cost per passenger-kilometer.
When fares climb to cover the costs, more passengers are
likely to drive or to discontinue travelling. If service to
low-intensity areas is to continue, subsidy is essential.

Subsidy for transit service in low-intensity suburban
areas is justified in several ways. It is defended as necessary
for traffic generation. Heavy traffic on the central city
routes, it is argued, requires good suburban service. This
argument implicitly recognizes the low probability for multiple
mode trips, a factor frequently ignored by transportation
planners. When passengers must drive to a stop and change
to public transit, they are likely to drive the whole way. In
all cities, the vast majority of public transit users live and
work within easy walking distance - about one kilometer - of
stops along transit lines. Few transfer from one public transit
line to another, and far fewer transfer from automobiles to
public transit. Transfers add to travel time and make
schedules uncertain.

To attract passengers, public transit provides more
suburban service than fare revenue can justify. The subsidy

is further justified on environmental grounds. The automobile is a source of accidents, pollution, and energy consumption problems, but it has many virtues from the driver's point of view - it is fast, it is comfortable, and it goes door-to-door. To entice passengers away from automobiles onto public transit, it is argued, public transit must match or exceed those virtues - it must be fast, service must be frequent, cars or buses must be comfortable, and fares must be low. Congestion in high-intensity areas means passengers in those areas require less enticement than those who travel in low-intensity suburban zones.

To capture suburban passengers, fares are kept low, and high-quality service is provided. The models discussed in Chapter 2 and observation of residential land use in cities shows that wealthier people live in suburban areas. The subsidy is for the group which has the option of driving. In the past 15 years, public transit subsidies have increasingly come from the United States federal government. Most federal funds are earmarked for capital investment. Cities buying new bus fleets or building new rail rapid transit lines budget with the expectation that the Department of Transportation will pay much of the bill. New buses purchased with federal funds have been assigned to suburban routes, both to attract passengers and because they are reliable and thus unlikely to break down far from the central bus garage.

Washington, D.C.'s Metro is the first rail rapid transit system to receive large federal subsidies. About 110 of Metro's proposed 150 kilometers are in low-density suburban areas where family incomes are high.

> Theoretically Metro could be of real significance for poor black people in the District of Columbia, those most in need of a rapid transit system. This will not be true, however, as the largest share of the benefits from Metro has been directed to the suburbs by a political structure in which the District of Columbia has virtually no political autonomy. Furthermore, the benefits to be realized by District residents do not align with the costs assigned them by a transit authority dominated by suburban members. The poor residents are being asked to expect the non-quantifiable benefits of Metro to "breathe new life into the District of Columbia" - non-quantifiable benefits which are doubtful at best.(1)

> William W. Brittain

BART was budgeted before substantial federal funds were available, but its planners did not assume that its capital would be raised at the farebox. The nearly $2 billion spent on building the lines and buying the cars were raised through state and local taxation, primarily with increases in sales and property taxes in the counties where BART lines are located. Economists consider those taxes regressive, that is the poor pay a higher share of their incomes than do the rich. Most of BART's lines and stations are in suburban areas housing middle- and upper-income people.

Public transit benefits do not accrue solely to riders. From the earliest days of mechanical transportation, lines have been built to promote real estate development. Extremely high-density land use as in New York and Chicago is possible because public transit lines bring hundreds of thousands to midtown Manhattan and the Loop each business day. It would not be possible to fill the high-rise offices with workers if buses, automobiles, and walking were the only means for commuting in those cities.

Real estate developers can now build 30-, 40-, and even 50-story office buildings along Market Street in San Francisco. Prior to BART, it would have been nearly impossible to fill the buildings with workers. The dramatic change in San Francisco's skyline has been accompanied by a huge increase in property values adjacent to some BART stations. High property values do mean higher real estate taxes (at least before Proposition 13) and thus a greater contribution to BART's cost.

While San Francisco's skyline has changed, automobile use in the San Francisco Bay Area remains high. BART was justified as a means of reducing traffic congestion, particularly on the Bay Bridge, and cutting air pollution. To date, the limited use of BART has cut automobile traffic imperceptibly if at all. Congestion and air pollution remain serious problems, as BART carries only half the number of passengers its planners predicted.

BART, like too many other public transit systems, presents a case of subsidies not matched by the benefits promised. While much of the subsidy comes from the pockets of the poor, most of the benefits fall into the pockets of major corporations and wealthy individuals. Major beneficiaries of bus investments include the manufacturers of buses and wealthy people in suburban areas who, for one reason or another, still use public transit service. One use is the reverse-commuting of domestic servants, who travel from their residential areas near the CBD out to the suburbs to work in the homes of the rich.

Much transportation planning has been mode-oriented, favorable to a particular type of public transit, usually rail rapid transit. It is intended to "provide an alternative to the

automobile," and at a minimum to "maintain existing service."
But is an alternative to the automobile really necessary? Is
the existing service necessary? Budget restrictons are forcing
transportation officials to ask those questions. Increasing
decentralization is making the automobile increasingly attractive
while reducing its adverse impacts. Lower congestion means
fewer traffic jams and less idling of car engines, a major
source of energy waste and air pollution. Moving jobs and
shops to the suburbs reduces the length of desire lines and
distances travelled, leading to further reductions of energy
consumption and air pollutant emission. Is it essential, or
even advisable, to maintain public transit from the CBD to the
suburbs when much of the population lives and works in the
suburbs?

Of course, not everyone can drive. The poor, the
young, the handicapped, and the elderly form the bulk of
present public transit users in the United States. How well
does public transit meet their needs? Suprisingly little
thought has been given to that question. Prior to the
automobile, a residence close to the CBD meant good access to
jobs, to shops, and to some types of recreation. The poor
and disadvantaged remain disproportionately concentrated in
residential areas close to the CBD, but today that location
often means little more than inexpensive, but low quality,
housing. The jobs, the shops, and the recreation facilities
have moved to suburban locations almost inaccessible to people
without automobiles.

TRANSPORTATION AND INEQUALITY

Merely living in a city does not ensure access to either
employment or services. A frustrating discovery by poor
migrants to cities is the lack of jobs, health care, education,
and even suitable shops in areas where housing is cheap. The
bright lights of Fifth Avenue or Michigan Avenue can be just
as remote to residents of Harlem and the South Side as they
are to people who remain in Alabama and Puerto Rico.

This remoteness is only partially due to transportation.
Cheap transportation from Harlem to Tiffany's is not going to
make luxury jewelry more available to the poor, nor, at a less
trivial level, is improved public transit to expensive private
hospitals (the typical kind of good hospital in the United
States) going to improve their medical care. In both instances, income is the key to access.

There are, however, strong links among income,
employment, and the availability of transportation. A steady
income is essential if people are to take advantage of living
in cities. The income can come from welfare payments, but

the evidence shows that most who are able to work want employment. In the poor neighborhoods of large cities, unemployment rates climb to as much as 50 percent of the potential labor force, with the highest rates of unemployment among the young. This unemployment can be attributed to such factors as attitudes, racial discrimination, and lack of education. In more than a few instances it reflects a simple lack of access to jobs, and inability to travel to the workplace.

In the concentric ring model, the poor cluster near the CBD because they are then close to many employment opportunities. Proximity to work means minimal expenditure on transportation. For those with the lowest levels of skill, it means access to a variety of possible jobs. Unskilled workers are often employed on a temporary or casual basis, and one job may last only a few weeks or just a few days. Street hiring of unskilled workers for a single day was a common sight in poor neighborhoods of American cities prior to 1940.

If the unskilled worker lives far from a concentration of jobs, unemployment is likely to be frequent, or a large share of earnings will need to be spent on transportation. From the viewpoint of those at the bottom of the income scale, any form of mechanical transportation is expensive. Ownership of an automobile with the costs it entails is usually out of the question. Public transit is the alternative, but fares can consume a large fraction of income. Public transit fares in most United States cities exceed a dollar for a return journey. Cash fares are lower in some European cities, but incomes are also lower.

An American worker earning minimum wage and using public transit to commute spends at least 5 percent of total earnings, and as much as 10 percent of take-home pay, on fares. In some European nations, the percentage is higher. A London secretary earning £ 50 per week with living accomodations five kilometers from work spends at least 40p per day on bus fares, 60p if the Underground is used. At £ 50 per week, the secretary is earning roughly the median income for British workers, half of whom earn less. The fares remain the same regardless of worker incomes.

For many workers, routes and schedules are as important as fares. The London secretary probably travels at rush hours, when buses and trains are frequent, if crowded. The worker who must arrive before 7 A.M. or return home after 10 P.M. rarely faces crowds (except in some East European nations and Spain) but may be forced to wait long periods for a bus or train. In some cities, public transit halts at night, and in most others, night service is infrequent. A missed bus means a long wait after an exhausting shift or an unpleasant wait on a bitter-cold winter night. Many night jobs require only limited skills and thus are open to the poor, if they can find a way to commute.

The combination of high fares and limited schedules makes certain jobs unattractive to potential workers. A worker forced to spend 10 percent of take-home pay and several hours each day commuting is likely to wonder if welfare payments might be a better source of income. If the unemployed in East Los Angeles were to use public transit for commuting to available jobs elsewhere in the city, up to 5 hours and round trip fares of $3-4 would be spent. Jobs in other parts of Los Angeles remain unfilled while unemployment in Watts and Boyle Heights is high. Given the structure of public transit, the jobs and the unemployed might just as well be in two different cities.

Los Angeles is, of course, the classic example of a multiple-nuclei city without a dominant CBD. It is also a city well adapted to the automobile. Lack of demand means public transit services are infrequent, and fares are high to cover costs of lightly used routes. The desire lines of few Angelennos coincide, and except on short routes, it is unusual for a bus to be filled. For the majority of the population who use automobiles, the public transit system is irrelevant. In no other large city can one find better facilities for automobile use. There is no need for public transit for trips into badly congested, high-density areas.

Los Angeles's dependence on automobiles is not without serious problems. Air pollution is the best known but perhaps not the most important. While a majority of the population own and drive cars, automobiles are not universally available, and it is difficult to provide adequate transportation for those unable to drive. The problem is especially acute in Los Angeles, since each of its clusters of economic activity specializes. The traditional CBD is today a center for government offices, banks, and corporate headquarters. It is neither the largest nor the most diverse retail center, and better public services, especially health care, are available at other centers. Needless to say jobs, and especially jobs for the unskilled, are also scattered into the various centers which are separated from each other by distances of about ten kilometers.

The choice of residence in Los Angeles, as in other cities, is limited for the poor. While multiple centers of employment have emerged, the residential pattern is still strongly focused on the older centers; in Los Angeles, sectors focused on the traditional CBD. Residential areas close to the CBD, originally built for workers, continue to offer the bulk of low-cost housing, as newer housing, close to decentralized employment centers, is more expensive and offered to the middle classes and the rich. Much of the newer housing has been built for sale, not for rental. Families at the bottom of the income scale rarely buy houses, and when they do the houses are generally older. The availability of housing means that the poor are clustered, though they might well desire to locate close to employment and not in a cluster.

An obvious, though partial, resolution of the problem would be greater provision of housing for the poor close to dispersed workplaces. In the recent past, most American cities, following court decisions and funding requirements of the federal government, have begun to make provision for low-income housing in areas away from the CBD. This is one type of land-use manipulation. Another type, virtually impossible under United States law, is the prohibition of decentralization. Only authoritarian nations, countries which allow individuals little freedom of choice in matters of housing and transportation, can effectively limit the outward movement of jobs away from the CBD. Most such countries, like the USSR and Sweden, have opted to encourage decentralization.

Provision of private transportation is an alternative which has received too little consideration. Might it not be better to provide transportation specifically for those groups who cannot normally drive, transportation comparable to the automobile? Several pilot projects suggest that it might well be better. One experimental program in England allows handicapped people who cannot drive standard automobiles a chance to buy and drive specially equipped vehicles, thus gaining mobility otherwise denied them. The huge costs of public transit subsidy suggest that it might be as cheap (or cheaper) to subsidize taxi service for those who cannot drive.

Merely improving transportation is not going to remove the problems of poverty, but it can mitigate some of them. The transportation problems of the disadvantaged minority result from land-use patterns which have evolved to suit the transportation demands of the majority. The overcrowded slums of the early industrial era were also a response to transportation. They provided access at the cost of horrid living conditions. Today the poor, on average, live much better, but many still lack access to jobs and services which might allow an escape from poverty. In Third World cities, the poor have the dismal prospect of horrid housing and lack of access, as we shall see in Chapter 4.

4 Urban Transportation in Third World Nations

POPULATION GROWTH AND URBAN TRANSPORTATION

Will Mexico City have 30 million residents in 2000? If its population continues to grow at the present rate, it will grow to be the world's largest city by that year. The world's largest cities at present are New York and Tokyo, with about 16 million inhabitants each and low rates of population growth. Many factors are likely to slow or halt population growth before Mexico City reaches 30 million, but the rapid rate of increase points to a common experience in Third World cities. Urban populations are growing fast in Latin America, Africa, and Asia. In 1950 the majority of the world's urban population lived in the cities of Europe and the United States, but a large majority of the world's city dwellers will live in Third World cities in 2000.

Until 1950 most Third World cities were small. In that year, no city in black Africa had as many as one million people. By 1970 at least 15 African cities south of the Sahara had over 1 million residents. Latin America had five "millionaire" cities in 1950 and is expected to have 25 in 1980. The large cities of Asia contained about 20 million residents in 1950 but will have over 150 million people in 1980 (see table 4.1).

Total population growth is rapid in Third World nations. In some it approaches the biological maximum. Urban growth rates are even higher than national rates of increase. Nations grow primarily because of an excess of births over deaths. In cities this natural increase is augmented with immigration as people born in rural areas move to cities. For much of urban history, cities grew only through immigration. Cities were unhealthy, and urban death rates frequently matched or

Table 4.1. Median Annual Total and Urban Population
Growth Rates for World Nations, by Regions,
1970–1975

Region	Total Population Growth	Urban Population Growth
Africa South of the Sahara (33 nations)	2.6	5.8
North Africa and Middle East (17 nations)	2.8	5.0
Non-Marxist Asia (minus Japan) (17 nations)	1.9	4.8
Central America and Carribean (11 nations)	2.9	4.0
South America (10 nations)	2.8	3.9
Wealthy Nations (20 nations)	0.8	1.7

Source: Compiled from data in World Development Indicators
(Washington, D.C.: The World Bank, 1978).

exceeded birth rates. Improvements in public health have
made Third World cities healthier than their rural areas. In
cities people have access to doctors and other health personnel, there is usually potable water, and disease-breeding
wastes are removed. At present Third World cities are
growing both through natural increase and immigration.

In the wealthy nations, by contrast, immigration is a
negligible factor of total urban growth. The reason is simple.
In Europe and North America, cities already contain 70 percent
or more of the population. Migration alters the relative sizes
of cities as people move from one city to another, but it does
not change the size of the total urban population. In the
larger Latin American nations 50 percent or less live in cities,
and in several African nations, less than 25 percent of the
population is presently urban. Rural areas contain a large
number of potential migrants.

Migration to cities is an ancient process. For generations people have been drawn from rural areas, and the attraction can be summarized in the word "opportunity."

The city is the metropolis of hope and desire, and universal variety of movement. . . It is the focus of the potentially productive mingling of classes and commerce; of enterprise and achievement.(1)

David Selbourne

Almost without exception, the best jobs are in cities, and the average standard of living is higher in urban than in rural areas. Cities contain the theatres, the libraries, the schools, the hospitals, and the well-stocked shops. Aspiring artists, politicians, and tycoons come to cities to make their fame and fortune, while peasants migrate with the hope of finding a steady income and a decent standard of living.

Upon arrival more than a few migrants are disappointed, but many others find what they seek. It is important to remember that even people forced to live in the most appalling urban poverty may be better off than they would have been if they had remained in a rural village. Though life in the city offers poor subsistence and little comfort, it is better than the endless toil and near starvation which are the lot of too many rural dwellers.

Opportunity has long been a magnet drawing people to cities, but until the nineteenth century, the migration stream was small. The costs and risks of the migration outweighed its benefits for most rural dwellers. During that century, abetted by transportation improvements such as the railroad, cities in Europe and North America attracted large numbers of migrants. Reductions in the cost of trans-Atlantic travel brought migrants from all parts of rural Europe to the cities of North America. From 1800 to 1910, urban growth rates in Europe and North America were high.

Just as transportation improvement drew people to European and North American cities, transportation improvements are encouraging migration to Third World cities. Since 1900, and especially since 1945, there has been massive investment in long-distance roads and railroads throughout the Third World. Though far from matching transportation needs, the new routes have cut travel times from weeks to days and hours. They have made rural residents more aware of urban opportunities, and they have cut travel costs to a level that many more people can afford. Several transportation projects in Third World nations have been blocked by a fear that they would unleash a flood of migrants and send them streaming toward unprepared cities.

Few cities have ever been prepared to deal with rapid immigration. Scarcity of resources and of the time required to provide housing and public utilities inevitably lead to strains, even in wealthy nations. This has recently been apparent in the cities of Florida. Lack of preparation has mean housing shortages, water-supply and sewage-removal problems, and a general overuse of public utilities.

Transportation is one of the overused public utilities. Time is needed to extend and expand a transportation system even when money is unlimited. When population growth is rapid, money for transportation is likely to be acutely limited. Housing, water supply, and sanitation are more directly related to public welfare and have a higher priority for funds. Housing is a particularly popular expenditure politically and thus is likely to capture a large share of available funds.

Housing, as we have already seen, is strongly linked to transportation. Housing is not useful unless it is accessible to jobs and services. Migrants are most likely to be at the bottom of the income scale, requiring inexpensive housing and cheap transportation. As cities grew in the United States and Europe during the nineteenth century, poor migrants were housed near the CBD. The housing was old or of poor quality and densities were high, but prices were low. The location allowed most trips to work, to shop, and for other purposes to be pedestrial. The concentric zone model was developed at the end of a period of rapid immigration to American cities, and the large numbers of recent migrants living close to the CBD were important to it.

The concentric zone model was first proposed when even the largest European and American cities were much smaller than many Third World cities today. In addition income levels were higher and public transportation systems were already more extensive. In 1920, Chicago housed barely 3 million people. Today Calcutta and Chicago are about the same size, 7 million, but present income levels in the Indian city are far below those of Chicago in 1920, and the capacity of Calcutta's public transit system is about that of Chicago's in 1900.

Population densities are very high in many Third World cities, upward of 50,000 per square kilometer in some instances. Pedestrian cities in Europe and North America were also high-density, but it was rare for their total population to exceed one million. The limit on total population meant a limit on land area and on distances within the cities. Even at high densities, large amounts of land are needed for housing in cities with three million or more residents, and the greater the amount of land used, the longer are the distances within the cities.

Distances are further increased by the land-use patterns common in Third World cities. Many of them are products of the European colonial era and bear marks of their origins.

Vast amounts of space in their centers have been left in parks
or devoted to monumental public edifices. At the time they
were laid out, few could envision their rapid growth, and
since most date from times after the railroad, it was assumed
that mechanical transportation would be available for their
residents. Even the oldest colonial cities were spacious, and
they were laid out for the benefit of the wealthier classes, who
were presumed to dominate their populations.

The cities have grown large, but they have not seen an
accompanying extension of transportation facilities. Resources
have not been available to invest in tracks and vehicles. The
monumental character of the CBDs and the lack of
transportation have kept wealthier residents close to the
center, unlike the rich who moved out from the center of
North American and European cities. This has severely limited
the housing available close to the CBD for poor migrants.
They have been pushed outward ever further from its jobs and
services. And even when public transportation is available, it
is likely to be erratic and expensive, beyond the means of
many poor people.

TRANSPORTATION AND HOUSING

Few writers on the problems of Third World nations fail to
discuss the terrible housing of the urban poor. Shanties built
of cardboard and oil tins, unserved by water or sewer lines
(let alone electricity or gas), with families crowded into spaces
of four square meters are all too common in the cities of
Africa, Asia, and Latin America. Half or more of all city
dwellers in Third World nations live in housing which would be
considered substandard in North America or Northern Europe.
Much of the housing is considered unfit for human habitation
by the governments of the nations where is is found.

It is not necessary to further describe the physical
quality of such housing here, but the location of housing for
the poor is of great importance in any discussion of
transportation in the Third World cities. We have already noted
the lack of adequate housing close to the CBD. In cities as
large as Calcutta, Cairo, or Mexico City it would be virtually
impossible to house all of the poor within walking distance of
the CBD. The poor are so numerous that housing at the
necessary densities is technically not feasible. If it were
possible, such a large area of very high density housing would
be likely to cause social problems far more serious than the
transportation problem it would resolve.

Many of the poor must be housed beyond walking distance of the CBD, most finding housing four or more kilometers away. Two of the reasons have been mentioned above:

occupancy of land close to the CBD by the rich, and the sheer numbers of poor people to be housed. At least two other factors are at work. First, considerable amounts of employment are located away from the CBD, and second, the agencies for housing provision, formal and informal, favor large scale development which demands large land tracts. Those are usually found at the edge of the city.

The automobile is not the cause of decentralization in Third World cities, but modern technology, including the truck, is a major force pushing jobs outward from the center. The scattering of employment is a result of demands for large sites, sites needed for modern manufacturing facilities. Many of the firms choosing locations are branches of United States and European companies, and they favor the types of location selected by the parent companies at home. Large land tracts adjacent to express highways are sought, and that means locations well outside the area of dense development. Good highways are few in Third World nations, but those which exist are usually found at the edges of major cities. In some instances, firms select locations as much as 50 kilometers from the CBD, especially if transportation facilities are available.

A modern factory employs from several hundred to several thousand workers. In Third World nations, industrial workers, poor by American or European standards, earn substantially higher wages than the national average. The wage rarely allows purchase of an automobile, but it does lead to a demand for a higher living standard. With the poor public transit characteristic of most Third World cities, the manufacturing firm has incentive to locate so that workers can walk to work. If housing in the city is scarce and of low quality, the firm is likely to consider building housing for its workers, or at least the skilled personnel. This has further prompted selection of sites where large amounts of land are available. A common solution has been construction of a company town within truck delivery distance of a major city.

The Third World company towns are much like some places built much earlier in the United States and Britain. Pullman, Illinois, now a part of Chicago, and Gary, Indiana, are early prototypes of company towns at the edge of a large city. Both were built for reasons similiar to those now at work in the Third World, and in their early days, Pullman and Gary were seen as ideal worker suburbs. A few years after it was built, however, Pullman was the site of one of the bloodiest strikes in American labor history. The social problems of Gary are more recent but well documented in the popular press.

In Third World company towns, as in Pullman and Gary, the manufacturing firm is the chief provider of housing as well as jobs. The towns are too remote for commuting, so they must house workers and provide them with services. The company stores and company control of housing give the firm

great control over the lives of town residents. People shop at
the company store since it is too costly to travel elsewhere.
They stay at their jobs since no alternative employment is
available within reasonable commuting distance. The firm may
retain ownership of housing units, and a worker who quits or
is fired is also evicted. In cities with severe shortages of
jobs and housing, the company has immense control over its
workers.

Lack of alternate jobs is incentive to keep a job even
when it requires living in substandard housing. Those with
factory jobs and housing, though their opportunites are
circumscribed by company control, may consider themselves
fortunate in comparison to the mass of the urban poor. The
terrible housing conditions so often described in United
Nations publications are found in neighborhoods where many,
most, or all of the potential workers do not have regular
employment. Some of the squalid dwellings are "legitimate."
Usually rental units, they are in buildings and on land for
which ownership titles meet legal requirements.

A large fraction of the Third World poor live in
"squatter" or "self-help" settlements, in dwellings which are
illegal. The two names are emotionally charged; authorities
view the residents as squatters, while more sympathetic
observers view the housing as self-help. We shall use the
term "squatter" because it is more frequently encountered in
the literature on Third World cities, a literature largely
prepared by the authorities. By use of the term we mean no
disapprobation of those living in the housing.

There is a significant locational difference between
legitimate and squatter housing. Legitimate housing is most
frequently close to the CBD in the locations suggested by the
land use models. Squatter settlements are more likely to be in
remoter parts of the city. Forcible eviction is the usual fate
of those who dwell as squatters on land close to the CBD,
though at times they are allowed to remain on steep hillsides
or poorly drained sites unsuitable for other uses. There is
power in numbers, and it is more difficult to evict large
numbers of squatters than small groups. Large settlements
require large sites, sites likely to be available only at the
edge of the city. In some Latin American cities, squatter
settlements at the urban edge contain more than 100,000
residents.

Company towns, legally secure and based on an
employment center, resolve transportation problems. Squatter
settlements at the urban edge create them. Almost by
definition, jobs and services are limited in squatter
settlements. People living in the settlements may start small
workshops and stores, but some residents must travel beyond
the settlements for jobs and services. The remote
locations mean many squatter settlements are beyond walking

distance of urban jobs and services. Public transit is needed, but since the people are poor, it must be cheap.

Good transportation service to squatter settlements is rare. The settlements are illegal, and most exist in spite of acute hostility on the part of public authorities. In Brazil, Chile, and India, squatter settlements have been destroyed by bulldozers and flame throwers (sadly not always after all the residents have been evicted). A less brutal effort to destroy the settlements is refusal of public services, including public transit. When transit and other services are not available, those with some alternative leave for housing where services are available, laeaving behind the poorest and most disadvantaged.

Public authorities claim they simply do not have the resources to extend transportation services to squatter settlements, a claim with some merit. When located at the edge of the city, as much as 25 kilometers from the CBD, the settlements demand a large transportaton investment if the CBD is to be accessible. With limited budgets, it is not possible to provide either the vehicles or the labor and energy to operate them. In many Third World cities, it is difficult to fund existing transportation service without making provision for extensions of services.

Where public authorities fail to provide transportation, some private entrepreneurs have filled the void. Jitneys, like the famous decorated jeeps of Manila, discarded buses, and even lorries or trucks (the "mammy wagons" of Central Africa) are brought into service. The service is rarely luxurious, as attested by pictures of people with a perilous handhold clinging to an overcrowded bus, but it fills a demand. With the transportation at least some who live in settlements at the urban edge can travel to employment and services at the center.

ALTERNATIVES

There are no simple solutions to the problems of Third World nations, of which urban transportation is but one. Many scholars and officials would select economic expansion or population control as the best way to resolve many of the problems. With economic expansion, more money will eventually be available for transportation. If total population growth is slowed or halted, the demand for transportation should increase more slowly or become stable. In the case of urban transportation, though, population control is not likely to have an immediate impact. Rural to urban migration can continue urban populaton growth at a rapid rate even after total population growth is slowed.

A more direct solution to urban transportation and housing problems is to impose restrictions on urban growth. This can be accomplished directly by making it difficult or impossible for migrants to come to cities. It can also be accomplished indirectly when the reasons for migration are reduced. The chief incentive for migration is the opportunities offered by cities and not available in rural areas. Increasing rural opportunities should slow the flow of people toward cities.

Increasing rural opportunities is itself related to transportation. Factories locate in or near cities because of the port facilities, railroad lines, highways, and airports which facilitate the movement of goods. If industry is to be attracted to rural areas, then investment in transportation is necessary. Over half of India's villages are more than ten kilometers from a paved, all-weather road.

> In India, where roads are very poor, bullock carts may still be carrying more freight than railways. . . A continued rise in goods and passenger facilities is indispensible for economic progress. One difficulty, of course, is the heavy concentration of transport facilities in the urbanized areas. Until vast rural areas are brought within the network of improved transportation and distribution, regional inequalities will widen.(2)
>
> Gunnar Myrdal

In some African nations, only one village out of twenty can be reached by standard trucks and automobiles, and many cannot be reached even with special vehicles (jeeps, Land Rovers, etc.) during all or part of the year. Industrial firms cannot locate in those places.

Latin American experience has shown that improvement of transportation to rural areas can speed rather than slow the rate of rural-to-urban migration. The new transportation routes reduce the cost of migration and make it feasible for more people. Prior to good transportation, a potential migrant may have stayed, knowing that a move would be permanent. Now the person can return, after a short time if urban opportunities fail to materialize, or for brief visits to impress friends and relatives with the success brought by the move.

A brutal halt of rural-to-urban migration has been brought by forcing people to stay in rural areas. In India during the "Emergency" declared by Ms. Ghandi, the urban poor, some of them natives of cities, were herded together, placed on cattle trucks, and taken to places far outside cities, where they were locked in fenced enclosures. Freedom was promised only in the event of a return to rural villages.

There is even unconfirmed evidence that several nations, including India, have exterminated urban immigrants.

Thankfully most nations have adopted more humane approaches. Resources have been allocated to the construction of housing and the provision of transportation in cities. Resources do not go far when a simple family dwelling costs as much as $2,000, and a new bus, built to the most minimal standards, costs about $20,000. Used buses from German and Swiss cities are cheaper, but they cannot be expected to last as long.

Each bus has a maximum capacity of about 2,000 commuters per day, assuming a trip of five kilometers, very crowded running, and staggered work hours so that demand is spread and traffic congestion limited. If most workers start and leave work at the same hours, and if streets are badly congested, the actual number carried is a small fraction of that maximum. The number of passengers (though not the number of passenger-kilometers) is reduced if the average trip is much longer than five kilometers. Dispersed employment can reduce the distances travelled, but in Third World cities it has tended to increase distances. When housing is available near workplaces, the trip can be short, but as in Los Angeles, the poor have little housing choice.

Cheap housing in Third World cities is concentrated in a few locations, some far from employment concentrations. We have already discussed the remoteness of squatter settlements. Public housing projects are also pushed to the urban edge, often far from jobs. Housing projects built to increase housing supply, to improve housing quality, and as an alternative to squatter settlements, are usually quite large. Some critics have argued that the projects create more problems than they resolve, since they encourage rural to urban migration. Whether that is true or not, the demand for housing is so great that even huge projects are usually insufficient.

Large demand combines with the cost advantages of building large projects to favor public housing estates with hundreds or even thousands of dwellings. Economies of scale, as an economist would call them, mean that the greatest number of dwellings can be constructed with a fixed total budget if several hundred or more are built in the same area at the same time. Large estates can be built on urban renewal land close to the CBD, but, more often, large vacant tracts at the edge of the metropolitan area are utilized.

Frontera I is a massive undertaking to provide a new community for 250,000 low-income people in the Rio metropolitan area, many of whom are displacees from favela removal actions in the inner city. Regardless of living conditions in these favelas, their residents did have ready access to employment and whatever services were available. But Frontera will be 80 kilometers from the center of Rio de Janeiro in an area that lacks any industrial employment and social services. Although some employment centers are planned in the vicinity, the residential areas will be constructed first, and even the best estimates of nearby job creation are lower than the anticipated labor force. Thus arduous commuting is inevitable. The reason for the location was succinctly put by an official of the National Housing Bank: "This was the only area we could find of sufficient size where land costs were 2 cruzeiros per square meter, our maximum land cost for this type of housing. If we moved the project 40 kilometers closer to Rio, land costs would be 150 cruzeiros per square meter, and out of the question."(3)

Malcolm D. Rivkin

Sites adjacent to good public transit, when it exists, are likely to be in use already, so many public housing estates, like squatter settlements, are remote from public transit. The nearest bus or train stop may be a 20- or 30-minute walk, and from the stop, the ride to the CBD may take 40 minutes to an hour or more. Cases of estates located more than two hours' travel time from the CBD are not rare. When jobs and housing are scarce, estate residents make the long commutes, though they would certainly prefer to spend less time and money on travel to and from work.

When the budget allows, public transit lines can be extended to housing estates. Few estates have been built in remote parts of cities without a promise of improved transportation. The promise can take a long time to materialize, as residents have discovered. Residents of estates located 50 kilometers from Rio de Janeiro were promised improved transit into that city when the estates were completed before 1970. To date the transportation routes have not been developed.

An alternative to transportation improvement is further decentralization of employment. In most Third World nations, government is one of the largest employers, and it has direct control over the location of many workplaces. Its own bureaus and offices can be moved into or near public housing estates to minimize transportation demand. Factories operated by state-owned enterprises can likewise locate within or close to housing estates. In the end, of course, this creates government controlled company towns. One complaint not faced by companies, however, is the charge that instead of creating such places close to major cities, the government should locate its operations in more remote areas to reduce the flow of migrants rather than close to cities, where the jobs and housing encourage migration.

5 Future Urban Transportation

TECHNOLOGICAL FIXES

Readers of the popular press can be forgiven a belief that important forms of new urban transportation are just around the corner. Magnetic levitation and gravitational propulsion make good copy if not good machinery. A skeptical review of the proposals for new types of transportation in cities suggests that present technology with minor modification is likely to remain dominant well into the twenty-first century. When radical new technologies have been tested, they have failed to meet required specifications even after huge cost overruns. Many transportation panaceas of the recent past - turbine engines for automobiles, guideways, and monorail systems, for example - have quietly faded from general consideration after proving unworkable.

Public authorities choosing technology for new transit lines and the reequipment of existing ones have been understandably cautious. In Newcastle, England a rail rapid transit system scheduled to begin operation in 1979 will use "tried and proven" technology.

> The hallmark of Tyne and Wear Metro is well-tried technology.(1)
>
> Tony Aldous

The Tyne and Wear Metro network will use technology similiar to that used in a number of German cities' 10 to 15 years earlier. Much of the technology was in use before 1925. The Tyne and Wear cars are likely to be more comfortable than their predecessors, but they incorporate few new features.

The major new technology applied in Newcastle, already in use elsewhere, is for train control. Computers and sophisticated radio communication will reduce the possibility of accidents and long delays caused by congestion. Although details have not been decided, a computer-based fare collection system is also likely. Assuming the computer systems work properly (not a completely safe assumption based on the experience of other urban areas), management of the Tyne and Wear Metro should be better than that of older rail rapid transit systems.

From the passenger's point of view, better management should mean lower fares (important in Newcastle, since the government subsidy for operating costs is rigidly restricted), fewer delays, and slightly faster speeds. The maximum speed will be about the same as that on systems built 50 years ago, but several changes allow faster average speeds. The most substantial increases in average speeds have been achieved by placing stations further apart.

The less acceleration and deceleration (starting and stopping) which are necessary, the faster the trains run on average (and incidentally the less energy is required to run them, since starting and stopping require a great deal of energy). Reduction of the number of stations to increase average speed was first applied on the express lines of the New York City subways during the 1920s. Parallel to the local lines, the express lines make only about one-third as many stops. The high average speed of BART has been achieved by placing stations far apart, four kilometers on the average.

Early rail rapid transit lines, using electric traction, had stations one kilometer or less apart, as in central New York, London, and Paris. Operating speeds on such lines are limited to less than 50 kilometers per hour, while BART can operate at over 100 kilometers per hour on some stretches. There is a cost associated with the increase in speed: a loss of flexibility. Most people living or working along the older lines are within easy walking distance, one-half kilometer or less, of a station. Many people living or working close to the newer lines are more than one kilometer from a station - more than a 15- or 20-minute walk.

Increase in speed through loss of flexibility has also occured for automobiles. Unlike rail traffic, automobiles have an inherent directional flexibility, but in both cars and trains, operating speeds and energy consumption relate to the number of starts and stops. Congested city streets with many stop lights mean low operating speeds and high energy consumption per kilometer driven. The express highway reduces congestion and eliminates stop lights thus allowing automobiles to take advantage of their horsepower while reducing energy demands. Like rail lines, however, express highways limit directional choice and flexibility by allowing entry and exit at only a few places. Most drivers on express highways have had the frustrating experience of seeing their destination at the side of the road while being forced to travel several additional kilometers to the nearest exit. Highway safety engineers have determined that entrance and exit points on express highways should be at least three kilometers apart. Of course, passing the destination is an experience long familiar to rail passengers forced to wait for a station stop.

Increasing speed by reducing the number of stops has not required any significant technological change. Much of the new technology applied to urban trnsportation has been in the field of civil engineering. Reenforced concrete structures have become stronger, lighter, cheaper, and often more attractive as well. New techniques for bridge and right-of-way construction have kept costs reasonable, but they have not been essential for increases in speed. The existence of the new routes, rather than any new construction technology they incorporated, is the critical variable for increased speed.

The public transit vehicle and the automobile of 1935 were capable of speeds similar to those on present rail lines and highways. The vehicles of the 1980s promise to be mechanically similar to those of a half-century earlier. This does not deny the importance of technological improvements which have made trains, buses, and cars safer, more comfortable, and more efficient in energy use, but the modifications have been minor. Minor modifications on the horizon promise to further increase safety, comfort, and efficiency, while mitigating some adverse environmental impacts. Noise levels and pollutant emissions are both likely to fall. Substantial increases in operating speeds are most unlikely.

Equally unlikely is some entirely new mode for urban travel. Nothing seriously proposed meets the conditions that would cause existing modes to be supplanted. Speed, flexibility, and cost are the critical conditions. Increased speed has been fairly easy to achieve, but always with a loss of flexibility and usually at a high monetary and energy cost. Tracked vehicles with speeds upward of 500 kilometers per hour are technologically feasible, but they require expensive tracks, can have few stops, and create severe environmental problems which make them unsuitable for use within cities. The present speed limit for urban transportation is about 100 kilometers per hour, and it seems most unlikely to be increased by any significant amount in the next quarter-century. The costs exceed any forseeable benefits.

Directional flexibility has proved elusive. Indeed, there has been a tendency to reduce flexibility in order to increase speed. The automobile remains the most directionally flexible form of urban transportation, a not inconsiderable reason for

its widespread use. Public transit, both for technological and
passenger-load reasons, is far less flexible. Buses have more
directional freedom than rail transit, but to ensure passenger
loads, even buses must operate over fixed and limited routes.
Only taxis, the public transit use of automobiles, now offer
the same directional freedom offered by the private automobile.

One effort to increase the directional flexibility of public
transit has been the fashionable people-mover. People-movers
take several quite distinct forms. One is computer-scheduled
service using small vans or buses. In the Washington, D.C.
suburbs, such a system is presently being tested with special
emphasis on the transportation demands of the elderly and
handicapped. By dialing a special telephone number, service
can be ordered. A computer than calculates the best route to
pick up passengers and deliver them to their destinations.
Unlike standard bus lines, these services stop at passenger
homes rather than fixed stops, and they do not operate over
fixed routes or with fixed schedules. They are sometimes
called demand scheduled services. They are too new to judge
their long-term utility, but they may well prove useful in
providing transportation for those who cannot drive. Computer
problems have been difficult, for it is an immensely complicated
task to develop the programs needed for demand scheduling.

A second type of people-mover is of limited but
significant application to situations where people must be
transported over short distances, one to five kilometers.
These distances are too great for many people to walk, but
conventional modes may not be able to provide the needed
service. Large amusement parks and airports have installed
several different types of people-movers to provide such
transport. Small buses and vans have been the most common
vehicles, including the strange-looking buses transporting
passengers from terminals to planes at Washington, D.C.'s
Dulles Airport and Montreal's new Mirabel Airport. In
Dallas/Fort Worth's new airport and at Seattle/Tacoma Airport,
rail rapid transit lines connect terminals. Moving belts and
escalators are found in most large airports. Perhaps the best
known people-movers are found in large amusement parks,
transporting customers between parking lots, hotels, and
various entertainment attractions.

To date, few of these people-movers have been used
outside the specialized environments of airports, amusement
parks, and shopping centers. Los Angeles has proposed an
elevated rail line to serve its traditional CBD. If built, the
short line will connect stores, pedestrian malls, offices,
transportation terminals, and parking lots. There is some
doubt as to its necessity, for automobile congestion is not
serious in central Los Angeles, and there are ample parking
facilities. The proposal is part of a more general urban
renewal scheme. Cynics have suggested that the people-mover

is intended to be an attraction, a carnival ride, since it serves
no pressing transportation demand.

The limited application of people-movers can be partially
explained by their cost. Right-of-way construction costs
usually amount to well over a million dollars per kilometer, even
for surface lines, and are higher when elevated or subsurface
lines are built. In addition the cost of land, of vehicles, and
eventually of operation must be considered. Since distances
are short, fares must be kept low. Users have the alternative
of walking. Captive users at airports and amusement parks
have common points of origin and destination, and they do not
usually pay a direct fare. Instead the transit fare is included
in the admission or ticket price. In cities where people have
choices, and where origins and destinations differ, usage of
people-movers is much less certain.

In a more general view, costs are the chief
discouragement of all new forms of transportation technology.
Research and development (R & D) costs can amount to many
millions of dollars when a radically new idea is adopted. Little
R & D expenditure is needed when tried and proven technology
is adopted. New ideas can result in unforeseen operation problems. This was amply demonstrated by the few new technological ideas embodied in BART. Doors which failed to close,
or opened between stations, train control malfunctions which
caused speed increases instead of stops, and malfunctions
in ticket collection equipment all added substantially to the
operating costs of BART during its early years. Operating
problems can lead to revenue losses and can discourage
potential passengers from using the service. They can also
require unbudgeted capital investments. The caution of public
transit officials in adopting new technology is easy to
understand.

Perhaps the most important barrier to the adoption of new
technology is the large investment in existing transportation
facilities. Radical new forms require new rights-of-way and
are not compatible with existing roads and rails. New
rights-of-way are expensive to construct, and acquisition of
land in densely populated areas can be prohibitively costly.
One of the reasons the automobile spread so rapidly was its
ability to use existing streets and roads. It did not require
(at first) huge right-of-way investments. No recent proposal
for radical new technology has been based on existing
rights-of-way.

Most large cities in Europe and the United States contain
hundreds of kilometers of railroad tracks. Many of the tracks
carry only a few freight trains a week, while others have been
abandoned entirely. Using standard rail vehicles, as in
Newcastle, the lines can be converted simply, if not cheaply,
to passenger transit. In Toronto the government of Ontario
uses such rail lines for its commuter GO Trains and similiar

service has been proposed on old rail lines in many other North American cities. Abandoned railroad rights-of-way form a significant portion of BART's lines. The conversion is not without difficulties. Many of the old rail lines pass through warehouse and industrial districts which offer few jobs and even fewer housing units to generate traffic.

Existing facilities are a strong conservative force resisting new technology. Included is the widespread ownership of automobiles and of facilities for their use. Once an automobile is purchased, it is to the owner's advantage to use it. Depreciation and other fixed costs (license, taxes, and insurance) must be paid whether the car is driven several hundred kilometers a week or a year. Even with huge increases in operating costs (gasoline, oil, tires, etc.), it is generally advantageous for the car owner to drive rather than use other transit modes.

To attract present automobile users, a new technology must be superior; and it must be cheaper to build and operate than traditional public transit modes if public authorities are to approve construction. In the next twenty-five years, no such technology is likely to supplant existing modes. Ideas proposed for the cities of North America and Europe cannot compete with existing modes, and research and development costs for the new modes are well beyond the means of most Third World nations. In Third World cities, most transportation investment will be for traditional technologies. Mexico City is extending its commuter railroad services, while other Third World cities build new highways and buy new buses.

FUTURE LAND USE

While dramatic proposals for new transportation technology capture headlines, dramatic changes to land-use patterns are taking place. Too often conceived of as works of art, urban land-use patterns are tools for achieving economic goals and reflections of economic aspirations. As the economic goals of society change, land-use patterns also change. In the complex society of a wealthy nation, land-use patterns are sensitive to many factors, but especially to transportation and transportation changes. In wealthy nations land-use is adapting to the private motor vehicle.

The adaptation is not always welcome. People lament the loss of open space as the city spreads outward. Some resent the fact that a suburban life style, once reserved for the rich, can now be enjoyed by middle-income and even fairly poor people. Other observers are upset by the near abandonment of once thriving commerical and industrial areas,

areas which grew to importance during the railroad era. The
changes have been rapid, and people are resistant to rapid
change. Not a few ill-advised land-use regulations have been
enacted to halt or slow the change. These reactionary laws
are intended to keep the city as it used to be, to ignore the
needs of contemporary society.

As long as urban residents continue to favor road
transportation, land-use changes are going to continue until
the form of the city has adapted to the needs of
transportation. The automobile and the truck do not work well
in high-intensity environments. When people are free to
purchase automobiles, and when commercial enterprises are
allowed to use trucks, these are the vehicles of choice. Even
when petroleum products are sold for a dollar or more a liter,
as in Sweden, there is little reduction in the use of road
vehicles for essential trips. Vacation and recreational travel,
and unnecessary business use, are reduced, but people
continue to commute by automobile, while firms continue to
favor truck deliveries.

One way to reduce petroleum usage is to avoid driving in
congested environments. Given a choice, automobile commuters
generally favor jobs in suburban office and factory complexes,
where parking is ample and streets are uncrowded. Shoppers
drive to regional shopping centers or commercial strips rather
than to the CBD. Travel from a suburban home to a suburban
job or shop avoids congestion and it reduces trip length,
another way to reduce petroleum use. The result is a
suburban landscape with housing, employment centers, and
shopping facilities scattered over a large area. The intensity
of land use is low, the best of all environments for automotive
transportation.

Prohibition of low-intensity suburban development, when
not accompanied by a prohibition of automobile and truck use,
creates more problems than it resolves.

> The idea that increasing traffic congestion will
> discourage either the buying or the use of cars has
> always proved a powerfully misleading tool.(2)
>
>   William Plowden

The almost hysterical prejudice against the automobile common
among West European planners has led to strong controls on
commerical and industrial development outside existing
high-intensity zones. The planners argue that continuing to
concentrate jobs and shops in CBDs, and in a few new centers
with the same characteristics as older CBDs, people will be
induced to abandon driving and use public transit. In most
cases, prohibition of suburban development has been
accompanied by substantial investment in public transit to the
high-intensity employment zones.

As any visitor to Western European cities can testify,
public transit is widely used, with the heaviest use in the
largest cities.   The same visitor is likely to be impressed by
the terrible traffic congestion, air pollution, and parking
problems in those same cities.   The use of public transit is
less a result of its attractiveness than of a lack of
alternatives.   In all but the Scandinavian nations, automobile
ownership is much less common than in North America, and
as many as half of 211 families in some European cities do not
own automobiles.   The family with two or more cars is
unusual.   Without cars people are forced to use public transit.
High taxes, the lack of storage space, and similiar barriers to
automobile ownership keep poorer people from owning cars.
In spite of the barriers, automobile ownership is
spreading rapidly in Europe.   As automobile ownership increases, use of public transit is falling.   All countries of
Western Europe have seen substantial declines in public transit
usage since 1960, a drop which parallels North American
experience during the 1950s.   When the automobile was being
widely adopted in the United States and Canada, land-use
controls were flexible and in many cities almost nonexistent.
New land-use forms, such as the regional shopping center,
could be tried, and after they proved successful, they could
be widely adopted.
There is an upper limit on the number of retail areas a
city can support, and the success of regional shopping centers
was accompanied by a declining patronage of older,
public-transit-oriented retailing.   Some older retail centers
have been able to adapt by providing parking, but most are
located in environments where automobile use is difficult and
the cost of land for parking almost prohibitive.   Not a few of
these older centers have been abandoned by shoppers and
thus by shops.
Planning law in Western Europe has been written to avoid
this type of adaptation to the automobile.   Suburban retail
facilities have been restricted as to location and size,
restrictions which almost prohibit regional shopping centers.
The suburban centers which are allowed are usually based on
existing shopping centers, often remnants of the period when
the suburb was still a rural village.   Like the CBD itself,
these suburban shopping areas are characterized by narrow
streets and a lack of parking, and as in the CBD, use of the
automobile is difficult.
While public transit is available, shoppers prefer to
drive.   The preference is easy to understand when large,
heavy, or bulky items are included on the shopping list.   The
inevitable result of the automobile preference is traffic
congestion even in the suburban shopping areas; and an
excessive expenditure of time, money, and energy by
shoppers.   Prohibition of suburban location has kept many

stores in the CBD, but it has also resulted in severe traffic congestion, additional air pollution, and traffic safety problems in that zone.

European planners have been cognizant of this congestion, and one of their solutions has been the new town. First popularized by Ebeneezer Howard as "garden cities," his new towns were updated versions of the railroad era suburbs of United States cities. Each was to be a miniature version of the core city, with jobs, shops, and housing. Like the string of beads sprawl discussed in Chapter 1, the new towns were to be surrounded by open space. Excepting this latter characteristic, most suburban development in North America has been consistent with the new town design ideals set forth by Howard and his disciples.

Since World War II, new towns have been a key element in European urban development policies, especially in those countries with socialist governments. Like Howard, who wrote when the automobile was just a toy for the rich, the planners have designed most of the new towns around railroads and public transit, though ideally the places were to be small enough to allow pedestrian travel to work and to shop. The railroads and public transit links were to the large core cities of which the new towns were satelites.

The new towns have proved rather expensive and not very popular. The expense arose from the necessity to recreate facilities already available in the core city. The lack of popularity had many causes, not least the authoritarian way in which people were forced to move into them. As automobile ownership has become more widespread, the popularity of the new towns has increased. They provide the same advantages as the postwar suburbs of the United States. Although they were originally designed for automobiles, the emphasis on open space has kept intensity of land-use low and made new-town life attractive to automobile users. While few express highways have been built to the centers of European cities, many of the new towns are adjacent to high-speed highways. This has made the new towns attractive also to industrial firms depending on trucking.

For all the discussion and planning effort, the evolving pattern of land use in Western Europe is not too different from the pattern which began to evolve earlier in North America. On both continents, the key characteristics are low-intensity land use and multicentricity. Together they make the city a better place for automobile use, but a place where public transit does not work well. In Europe, as in North America, the public transit oriented CBD is loosing its attractiveness, with shops, factories, and even office buildings vacant. In Europe, as in North America, there is a problem with no easy solution - provision of transportation for those who cannot drive.

Land-use controls can slow the rate of change and they can influence the details of change, but they do not alter its basic direction. Many Americans have commented favorably on European new towns, contrasting them with the "slurbs" which surround cities in the United States and Canada. From an architectural viewpoint, the authoritarian land-use controls in Europe have had distinctive advantages, requiring design standards and the provision of amenities like open space. On the negative side, the controls have hindered changes which would make the city better suited to its dominant transportation mode. The controls have been conservative and have failed to anticipate change and the new demands and goals which stimulate it.

The most significant of the new demands relate to the rapid diffusion of the automobile. As more and more European families acquire the car, European cities must perforce adapt to it. If it is to be an efficient mode for urban transit, then city land use must be altered. Express highways and parking are necessary, and land-use intensity must be limited. Older neighborhoods which are too congested for automobile use may well fall into disuse. If we wish to keep the city as it used to be, then we must agree, or be forced, to abandon the automobile. Agreement is unlikely, and stronger force than any thus far applied is needed to cause people in wealthy nations to stop using cars for urban travel. In consequence we must expect to see continued land-use adaptation.

THE FUTURE OF THE AUTOMOBILE IN THE CITY

Unless its use is prohibited, the automobile will be the dominant mode of passenger transportation for the forseeable future. Western nations have committed too many resources to abandon cars; the changes to cities, to life styles, and to national economies have been too great for a reversion backward toward a pedestrian or rail transit society. No technology superior to the automobile in speed, flexibility, comfort, and cost has been put forth, and when it is, it will take years to replace cars, just as the dominance of the automobile came only gradually. Success of the mode which replaces the automobile will require further land-use changes. For the present, Western nations must learn to live with automobiles, a learning process most advanced in the state of California, often the bellwether of social futures.

The importance of automobiles in Third World cities is less obvious but equally great. Automobile ownership in Africa and Asia lags far behind even the poorest nations of Western Europe, but most of the cars are in cities. Rare is the Third World city without at least a few kilometers of express highway

and immense rush-hour traffic jams. Car ownership is limited
to higher-income people, those who have the power and
resources to mold societies and cities. Car ownership is a
mark of status, and it ranks near the top on the list of
desired consumer goods.

> A new man, he remained a stranger in Bombay, more
> of an outsider than any visiting European technician,
> to whom many doors are open. Malik qualifications
> for the young business executive or "box-wallah"
> society seemed high, but at our first meeting he told
> me of the probing by which he was continually
> rejected. That he was Scandivania returned was
> impressive. That he worked for an established firm
> with European connections made him more than
> promising. Then: "Do you own a car?" Malik didn't.
> The probing was discontinued; no one was even
> interested in his parentage.(3)

> V.S. Naipaul

In that sense, the Third World is similiar to Europe prior
to 1960 and North America before 1925, when car ownership
was largely restricted to the affluent and the powerful. One
might argue that these form a small fraction of the societies,
but it is the critical fraction. Even if widespread automobile
ownership is unlikely, cars do not need to be numerous to
have a profound impact on the pattern of urbanization.

The demands of the rich and the powerful have great
influence in the molding of land use. Railroads were initially
expensive and used for commuting only by the rich. "The
advantage of living in low-intensity environments, in sprawling
residential areas with much space per person, was first demonstrated by the rich." Their suburbs along the shore of Lake
Michigan north of Chicago, on Long Island Sound outside New
York City, and near the Main line of the Pennsylvania Railroad
near Philadelphia served as prototypes for the garden cities of
Ebeneezer Howard. Transportation development made a similar,
if less opulent, life style available to the middle income segment
of society which eagerly adopted it.

The rich were also first to demonstrate the advantages of
automobile use in cities. When mass production made cars
inexpensive, the spread was rapid. Lack of cheap,
mass-produced automobiles retarded their spread in Europe,
but there was a latent demand. To win popularity, Adolph
Hitler designed a "people's car" (Volkswagen), though few
were built until after World War II. In the recent past, rising
incomes and availability of inexpensive automobiles have rapidly
increased car ownership among the middle- and lower-income
groups in Europe.

Cheap automobiles have had a strong appeal even in some of the poorest Third World nations. In India a people's car project was started, but it was discredited during the Emergency and subsequently abandoned. It is unlikely that a car cheap enough for more than a small fraction of India's families can be built. On the other hand, development economists view the automobile industry as a key element in economic growth.

The role of the automobile industry in national economies is immense. It has been estimated that a quarter or more of the jobs in the American economy are strongly tied to automobile manufacture, maintenance, and use. In addition to car manufacturing (and the manufacture of steel, aluminum, fabrics, rubber, and other materials for automobiles), petroleum refining, sales of automobiles and gasoline, automobile repair, the travel industry, and a very large segment of retailing (e.g., fast foods) are directly dependent on cars. Automobile production and use has a potential propulsive effect, encouraging growth in many parts of the economy. While it is presently fashionable to condemn economic growth in wealthy nations, the growth related to automobiles has not escaped notice by economic planners in the Third World. The automobile industry has been fostered as a key to economic growth by several Latin American governments, even though its products are too expensive for much of the population. The automobile has played an important role in recent Brazilian, Japanese, and Korean economic growth.

Increasing automobile use may bring economic development. It undoubtedly brings problems. Two problems which have received a great deal of attention are safety and air pollution. A nation without cars is not completely safe nor is it free from air pollution, but needless death and injury, and foul air, increase as automobile use increases. In the past 30 years, the individual automobile has become safer and less polluting - there are fewer accidents and less pollutant emmission per kilometer driven. The increase results from more vehicles, drivers, and kilometers driven.

Among teenagers and young adults, automobile accidents are a major cause of death. It is beyond the scope of this book to investigate the causes of automobile accidents, but they include mechanical malfunctions, bad highway conditions, alcohol abuse, psychological distress, and even homicide. The problem of automobile accidents is most acute in cities which have failed to adapt to the car. When slow-moving local traffic and fast-driving through vehicles must share the same streets, there is conflict; one result is large numbers of accidents. Express highways which separate local traffic from through traffic inevitably reduce the conflict and the number of accidents.

Persons resisting the construction of express highways are often hailed in the popular press as community heroes, "friends of ecology." One result of their success is an increase in needless death and injury on city streets, not to mention property damage. The conflict between types of traffic is severe when pedestrians, slow and soft, must share the same streets with fast and hard automobiles. The failure to segregate pedestrians from cars and trucks makes city streets inefficient, unpleasant, and unsafe for both walkers and drivers. Segregating slow traffic from fast makes movement smoother as well as safer, reducing the number of stops and starts.

The laws of physics make frequent stops and starts inefficient, and the design of engines make them major generators of air pollution. Emmissions of nitrogen oxides, carbon monoxide, and unburned hydrocarbons are the lowest when travel is at a constant speed and greatest when stops, starts, and engine idling are frequent. Urban air pollution long predates the automobile. It was a problem in Shakespeare's London. Smog, a particular form of air pollution, is more closely associated with the internal combustion engine. Older forms of air pollution included much particulate matter, while smog is primarily gaseous, the brown haze which can be seen on the horizon when one travels from a rural area toward a large city.

Los Angeles, the city associated with smog, has no monopoly on it, and its metropolitan area was the first to adopt rigid measures to control automotive pollution emissions. However, measures have been only partially successful. Air quality in Los Angeles has not deteriorated in spite of increased automobile use, but Los Angeles air is unsafe to breathe on some summer days. It is not correct to blame the car alone, however. Los Angeles is simply too large for its environmental resources. It must draw water from the Owens Valley, the Colorado River, and the Sacramento River, all hundreds of kilometers away, and its air supply is too small for the number of people and the mix of activities it contains. Los Angeles is in no sense unique, for most large cities exceed local air and water supplies in their demands for those resources.

Proper emission controls can reduce automobile-generated air pollution to tolerable and even negligible levels in small and medium sized urban areas. The high concentration of automobiles and pollution-creating activities makes the reduction almost impossible in very large cities. Until there is a technological revolution, poor air quality is going to be endemic over the world's largest cities, even if automobile use is banned. Other forms of transportation, power generation, manufacturing, and home heating systems will insure poor air quality when many of them are crammed onto small amounts of land.

The large city is not a creation of the automobile but rather of older transportation modes, in particular the railroad. Like rail public transit within the city, railroads demand large concentrations of users in few locations. The immense concentration of manufacturing near the rail yards of Chicago illustrates this demand. Only through the clustering of factories and warehouses near a few terminals could the railroad companies be assured of adequate traffic. The concentration of economic activities, in turn, required a concentration of population to provide the necessary labor, and the result was the large city, a product of the railroad era.

The truck and the automobile have greatly reduced the need for large cities. The movement of manufacturing from central city rail yards to suburbs, and increasingly to small cities, has been a consequence. Such decentralization disperses pollutant emissions over larger areas and reduces smog. For photochemical smog to form, it is necessary for a substantial quantity of the various pollutants to collect within a small volume of air. The necessary concentrations are unlikely in the air over small cities.

To live in the environment of small cities is an express desire of many Americans as demonstrated by public opinion polls.

> Given today's level of American affluence and technology, it is quite possible to have a metropolitan area without much of a central city. We no longer need very large cities to transact most business, and by their recent migration Americans have shown an aversion to living in most of them. The rich and most of the middle class have the wherewithal to live where they choose, and increasingly they have demonstrated a preference for more space, greenery, and tranquility than is to be found in obsolescent, crime-plagued central cities.(4)
>
> Gurney Breckenfeld

People like the high wages and services of the large cities, but they prefer to live in the more spacious, less crowded confines of small cities. With the automobile, it is possible to have the best of both, life in uncrowded suburbs and even small cities with access to the services and the jobs of large cities. In the past decade, much of the American population has voted with its feet, moving to smaller urban centers. Some of the largest cities, especially those in the Northeast and Midwest, have lost population. Buffalo, Cleveland, Pittsburgh, and New York have fewer people today than in 1970. Other large cities have gained only a few, while some small cities have nearly doubled their populations.

For automobile users, smaller cities have distinct advantages, including lack of congestion and short distances between activities. Recreational driving is a major leisure activity. A short drive takes one well outside a small city, while an hour or more of driving may be needed to reach the edge of a large city on a weekend drive into the country. With high gasoline costs, residents of large cities are likely to abandon recreational driving. Too much petroleum is needed for necessary travel within the city to afford the long trip to the city edge and beyond. The necessary use of energy in small cities is less, so pleasure driving can continue, if at a reduced level.

Smaller cities have distinct disadvantages for those who do not drive. They rarely contain a wide range of shops selling specialized goods and unusual services. Their populations are too small to support out-of-the-ordinary commerce. Few travel desire lines coincide, so public transit service, if it exists, is infrequent. Access to the services of a major city may be impossible unless one drives, for the quality level and problems of the intercity bus and rail services are well known. Life in a small city can be pleasant for those who drive but most uncomfortable for those who do not.

The movement toward smaller cities is made possible by increased use of automobile and truck transportation. Without such use, continued growth is possible only in a restricted number of large cities. This is the case in much of the Third World, where automobiles and trucks cannot be expected to meet more than a small part of transportation demand. The truck is allowing growth of some smaller cities, but the lack of good roads means that, for the present, even truck-dependent industry must locate fairly close to the biggest cities. Only with massive investment in new highways is there much hope for scattering the activities into smaller places.

As long as residents must continue to use public transit, there is little chance for the reduction of the size and crowding in Third World cities. As Third World nations become wealthier, they may have a chance to adopt automotive transport and avoid some of the problems faced in the largest cities of Europe and North America. It seems more likely that they will simply repeat the experience, creating excessively large cities with terrible problems related to crowding and to overuse of the physical environment. For most Third World cities the future is bleak.

In Europe and North America, the urban future promises to provide ever larger portions of the population with the kind of urban life they desire. At the same time, it offers a good chance of reducing the environmental problems associated with automobiles and cities. The price is an almost total dependence on a single mode of transportation for passenger movement - the automobile. In much of the United States

and Canada that dependence already exists. No alternative
mode presently available can possibly supplant the automobile
without requiring massive alterations to life styles and land
uses.   Commitment to the automobile is complete, and until
there is a technological revolution in passenger transportation,
it is irrevocable.

SUMMARY

Transportation in cities has long been a major human problem,
and it promises to remain one for the foreseeable future. In
the past two centuries, people have discovered means to
overcome one part of the urban transportation problem –
moving food, fuel, and raw materials into cities and moving
products   and   wastes   out.   Improvements   to   goods
transportation have allowed the growth of ever larger cities,
and with urban population growth, the problem of passenger
transportation has become paramount. In the contemporary
city, the movement of people from home to work, to shop, to
play, and back again is the transportation problem.
     Transportation of people within cities was not a problem
when cities were small and when integrated patterns of land
use made distances between activities short.   The development
of mechanical transportation encouraged the spreading growth
of cities and the segregation of land uses, increasing distances
and requiring the use of vehicles for necessary travel.   The
strong   relationships   between   transportation   and   land-use
patterns   are   an   important   factor   in   understanding   urban
transportation problems.   The land-use pattern of a city
adapts to the type of transportation which is dominant.
     In the cities of twentieth-century North America and
Western Europe, the dominant transportation mode is the
automobile, and cities have been reorganized to allow its use.
Failure to adapt to the automobile, and in particular failure to
control density and allow multi-centered development lead to
many of the problems associated with automobile use in cities:
smog, safety hazards, and excessive energy consumption.   The
problems can be minimized if the urban land-use pattern is
allowed to adapt to the needs of automotive transportation.
     The price is an almost total dependence on the automobile
for movement within cities.   For most of the population, that
presents no problem, but part of the population is too young,
too old, too poor, or otherwise unable to drive.   Provision of
transportation for those people is a major social problem, and
one which has not received sufficient attention as a vast
portion of public transportaton subsidies go to provide
underutilized services to wealthy neighborhoods.

Providing transportation for the disadvantaged is also the major problem of many Third World cities. With rapidly growing populations, the cities of Africa, Asia, and Latin America are finding it difficult to provide the bare essentials for urban survival. Inadequate transportation is endemic as potential workers find it impossible to travel to jobs and rural migrants find levels of social services in the city only slightly better than those of poor and remote regions. Continued growth of Third World cities offers little hope for resolution of transportation problems anytime soon.

It is clear that transportation development in those cities will be based on existing types of transportation. Even in the poorest, the automobile will play a dominant role, and in the wealthy nations, the automobile will dominate the city for the foreseeable future. Other technologies are too expensive, too inflexible, or too inconvenient to replace the fairly cheap, fast, and convenient car as the preferred means of urban transportation. If the automobile is to work well in cities, however, cities must adapt to its demands, including low overall land-use intensity and integration of functions. The very large city is a poor environment for automobile use. The car works much better in a small city, in exactly the kind of urban environment where a majority of Americans indicate they would like to live.

Notes

CHAPTER 1

1. Fernand Braudel, The Mediterranean and The Mediterranean World in the Age of Phillip II, trans. Sian Reynolds (London: Fontana/Collins, 1966, 1972), pp. 385-386.
2. Karl Marx, Capital: A Critique of Political Economy, trans. Friedrich Engels (London: Swan Sonnenschein, Lowrey and Co., 1877), vol. 1, p. 618.
3. Ian B. Thompson, The Paris Basin (Oxford: Oxford University Press, 1973), p. 21.

CHAPTER 2

1. B. T. Robson, Urban Analysis (Cambridge: Cambridge University Press, 1969), p. 9.
2. Friedrich Engels, The Condition of the Working Class in England (Moscow: Progress Publishers, 1970, reprint).

CHAPTER 3

1. Willard W. Brittain, "Metro: Rapid Transit for Suburban Washington," in David M. Gordon, ed., Problems in Political Economy: An Urban Perspective (Lexington, Massachusetts: Lexington Books, D.C. Heath and Company, 1971), p. 443.

CHAPTER 4

1.   David Selbourne, An Eye to India (Harmondsworth,
Middlesex: Penguin Books, 1977), p. 48.
2.   Gunnar   Myrdal,   Asian Drama: An Inquiry Into the
Poverty of Nations, abr. Seth King (Harmondsworth, Middlesex: Penguin Books, 1971), p. 86.
3.   Malcolm D. Rivkin, Land Use and the Intermediate-
Size City in Developing Countries (New York: Praeger Publishers, 1976), p. 15.

CHAPTER 5

1.   Tony Aldous, "Supertram (2): Metro's Well-Tried
Technology," New Scientist, 76, No. 1081 (8 December 1977):
630.
2.   William   Plowden,   The Motor Car and Politics in
Britain (Harmondsworth, Middlesex: Penguin Books, 1971), p.
337.
3.   V. S. Naipaul, An Area of Darkness (Harmondsworth, Middlesex: Penguin Books, 1964), p. 52.
4.   Gurney Breckenfeld, "Refilling the Metropolitan
Doughnut," in The Rise of the Sunbelt Cities, David C. Perry
and Alfred J. Watkins, eds., Urban Affairs Annual Reviews,
vol. 14 (Beverly Hills, Calif.: Sage Publications, 1977), p.
240.

Glossary

Central Business District (CBD) The area at the core of the city where offices and retail stores use most of the land. It is usually the oldest part of the city, and at its edge are major transportation terminals such as bus stations and railroad depots.

Commuting Travel between a person's place of residence and his or her place of work.

Desire lines Links between passenger places of origin and destinations drawn on a map. When mapped, desire lines show the demand for transportation services over various routes.

Economies of scale The relationship between the size and the cost of operation of an activity. For most activities the cost of operation decreases as size becomes larger to some optimal size, and above that size the cost increases as size becomes larger.

Functional integration The mixture of various types of urban activities including housing, manufacturing, and retailing in a small area, sometimes in a single building. Contemporary United States cities are characterized by functional segregation with each of the types of activity separated into distinctive regions of the city.

High intensity land use The concentration of a great amount of activity or a large number of people into a small amount of space. Land use intensity is usually measured in terms of population density, or it is expressed in terms of land values.

Isotropic surface An undifferentiated area on which travel is equally difficult in all directions, and the cost of transportation is solely a function of distance. On an anisotropic surface various conditions make travel less difficult in some directions than in others, and the cost of transportation is a function of both distance and direction.

Leapfrog sprawl Development at the edge of cities which mixes patches of urban development with tracts of land still in rural uses. Initially it occurred with railroad suburbs, but more recently it has resulted from automobile use and, in Europe, from new town development.

Mode oriented transportation planning The design and development of urban passenger movement systems favoring one particular type of carrier, often rail rapid transit.

Model A simplified representation of reality. Models serve as the base for explanation and analysis of complex phenomenon such as the relationship between transportation and urban land use.

Passenger-kilometer The movement of one person a distance of 1,000 meters (0.62 miles).

People mover Any of several types of transportation modes designed to carry small numbers of passengers or to transport them over short distances.

Regional shopping center The suburban shopping mall, a retail selling area which has been planned and usually contains several department stores and a number of more specialized stores.

Reverse commuting The movement of poor people from residential areas near the CBD to jobs in suburban locations.

Bibliography

The literature on transportation and urban land use is large and growing rapidly. The list below is a tiny selection from that literature, a sample selected for its readability and its relation to topics raised in this book. Most of the titles in the list below contain bibliographies which can be consulted by the reader who wishes to delve more deeply into the topics.

Blumenfeld, Hans. The Modern Metropolis: Its Origins, Growth, Characteristics and Planning. Cambridge, Massachusetts: MIT Press, 1967.

Edited by the architect Paul Speiringen, this collection of essays presents some provocative and insightful material on the nature of cities and their future prospects. Of particular interest are the essays on the relationship between transportation and urban form and the papers on the future forms of transportation in the city.

Bourne, Larry S., ed. Internal Structure of the City: Readings on Space and Environment. New York: Oxford University Press, 1971.

A general collection of essays on the form of cities, this reader includes most of the classic papers on urban form and many writings on the relationships between land use and transportation in the cities of North America and Europe.

Clark, Colin. "Transportation: Maker and Breaker of Cities," Town Planning Review. 28 (1958): 237-250.

Clark's paper is an important short statement about the relationships between transportation and urbanization.

Creighton, Roger L. Urban Transportation Planning. Urbana: University of Illinois Press, 1970.

Although somewhat dated, this book is still the most widely used textbook for training urban transportation planners. It is an excellent compendium of the ideas, techniques, and mythologies which guide (or misguide) the design and operation of urban transportation facilities.

Dyos, H. J. and Aldcroft, D. H. British Transport: An Economic Survey from the Seventeenth Century to the Twentieth. Leicester, England: Leicester University Press, 1969. (Also published as a Penguin paperback.)

Transportation change has been a key element in the development of modern Britain and its cities. Dyos and Aldcroft provide a readable history of the transportation changes and their impacts, a history which has many parallels to the experience of other western nations.

Flink, James J. The Car Culture. Cambridge, Massachusetts: MIT Press, 1975.

Flink's fascinating book is a general overview of the process by which the automobile has been adopted into American culture and the effects the car has had on the "American way of life."

Gakenheimer, Ralph, ed. The Automobile and the Environment: An International Perspective. Cambridge, Massachusetts: The MIT Press, 1978.

One of the few publications to deal with the role of automobiles in Third World countries, this collection of papers is concerned wth the role and problems associated with the use of automobiles in contemporary cities. In spite of its title, it is concerned with far more than the relationship between cars and the environment.

Hamer, Andrew. The Selling of Rail Rapid Transit: A Critical Look at Urban Transportation Planning. Lexington, Massachusetts: Lexington Books, D.C. Heath and Company, 1976.

While somewhat more technical than the other items in this bibliography, Hamer's study can be recommended as one of the best and most thorough analyses of the costs and benefits which accompany urban rapid transit. Even skipping the detailed economics, there is much to be learned from this book.

Lowe, John and Moryadas, S. The Geography of Movement. Boston: Houghton-Mifflin, 1975.

This book provides a survey of transportation geography and includes extended presentation of the tools which can be used to analyze transportation systems.

Mayer, Harold M. "Cities: Transportation and Internal Circulation." Journal of Geography. 68 (1969): 390-405.

A short but concise article outlining the relationships between transportation to cities and transportation within cities as they apply to the urban land use pattern.

Nelson, Howard and Clark, William A. V. Los Angeles: The Metropolitan Experience. Association of American Geographers Comparative Urban Analysis Project. Cambridge, Massachusetts: Ballinger Publishing Company, 1976.

Los Angeles, called by one writer the "Ultimate City" and by cynics "a thousand suburbs in search of a city" is the oldest and largest of the automobile-dominated cities. This brief book surveys the present pattern of land use in Los Angeles, and its implications.

Owen, Wilfred. The Accessible City. Washington, D. C: The Brookings Institution, 1972.

A problem statement for a large-scale study of urban transportation needs and resources, Owen's book focuses on difficulties of movement within cities and some of the ways in which those difficulties can be resolved.

Owen, Wilfred. The Metropolitan Transportation Problem. Washington, D. C.: The Brookings Institution, 1966.

One of the earlier statements on difficulties of movement within cities, this book had a significant impact on transportation analysis and planning during a period when large sums were being spent on urban transportation facilities.

Rae, John. The Road and the Car in American Life. Cambridge, Massachusetts: MIT Press, 1971.

Rae has written a compelling history of the automobile and its influence on various aspects of American society. He is a foremost authority on the history of the automobile in America, and his other books and papers on the subject are also highly recommended.

Roads and Transportation Association of Canada. Urban Transportation Planning Guide. Toronto, Ontario: University of Toronto Press, 1977.

Not meant for casual reading, this book is a compendium of techniques for the analysis and design of urban transportation systems.

Taebel, Delbert A. and Cornehls, James V. The Political Economy of Urban Transportation. Port Washington, New York: Kennikat Press, 1977.

In this book the authors attempt to relate the problems and proposals of urban transportation to the broader concerns of American social and political organization.

United Kingdom, Ministry of Transport. Traffic in Towns. London: HMSO, 1963.

This is the best known and most influential work yet written on urban transportation. It is usually called the "Buchanan Report" after its principal author Colin Buchanan. In retrospect many of the ideas it contains can be shown to be wrong, but it has been a major influence on urban transportation planning in the United Kingdom and elsewhere.

Webber, Melvin M. "The BART Experience--What Have We Learned?" The Public Interest. 45 (1976): 79-106.

Webber was one of the planners responsible for the layout of the rapid transit system in the San Francisco Bay Area. This article is a critical evaluation of BART and a mea culpa.

Wheeler, James O. The Urban Circulation Noose. North Scituate, Massachusetts: Duxbury Press, 1974.

Like many writers on urban transportation, Wheeler has a distinct bias against the utilization of automobiles in the city. The book discusses urban transportation problems with and emphasis on those created by the automobile, especially the problem of access for the economcally disadvantaged.

Yeates, Maurice and Garner, Barry. The North American City. 2nd ed. New York: Harper & Row, 1976.

The second half of this basic and comprehensive text on urban geography begins with an excellent chapter on transportation and city land use. The last sections of the book provide concise and readable summaries of various aspects of urban land use.

   In addition to the books listed above, the reader may
wish to look at some of the many periodicals which occasionally
contain papers on transportation and urban land use.   All of
the major journals in economics, geography, sociology, and
city and regional planning occasionally publish papers related
to the concerns of this book.   Several journals such as
Traffic Quarterly,   Transportation Research   (Part   A),   and
Transportation Engineering are multidisciplinary and contain a
number of papers on transportation in cities.

Index

About the Author

ELDOR PEDERSON (Ph.D., University of California, Berkeley) is currently Associate Professor of Geography and Regional Science at George Washington University in Washington, D.C., where he has been on the faculty since 1970. He has also taught at Sonoma State College and San Francisco State University. During a sabbatical leave in 1977-78 (while this book was being written) he lectured at Portsmouth Polytechnic, the University of Liverpool, and Oxford University in England. His past research has focused on historical aspects of transportation and urbanization, while his current research project concerns land use and transportation demands in the present-day cities of South and Southeast Asia.